THE INCREDIBLE ADVENTURES OF LOUIS RIEL

THE INCREDIBLE ADVENTURES OF LOUIS RIEL

Canada's Most Famous Revolutionary

HISTORY/BIOGRAPHY

by Cat Klerks

For my parents

PUBLISHED BY ALTITUDE PUBLISHING CANADA LTD.
1500 Railway Avenue, Canmore, Alberta T1W 1P6
www.altitudepublishing.com
1-800-957-6888

Extreme care has been taken to ensure that all information presented in
this book is accurate and up to date. Neither the author nor the
publisher can be held responsible for any errors.

Publisher	Stephen Hutchings
Associate Publisher	Kara Turner
Series Editor	Jill Foran
Editor	Pat Kozak
Digital photo colouring & maps	Scott Manktelow

We acknowledge the financial support of the Government
of Canada through the Book Publishing Industry Development
Program (BPIDP) for our publishing activities.

Altitude GreenTree Program
Altitude Publishing will plant twice as many trees as were used
in the manufacturing of this product.

National Library of Canada Cataloguing in Publication Data

Klerks, Cat
The incredible adventures of Louis Riel / Cat Klerks.

(Amazing stories)
Includes bibliographical references.
ISBN 1-55153-955-1

1. Riel, Louis, 1844-1885. 2. Red River Rebellion, 1869-1870--Biography.
3. Riel Rebellion, 1885--Biography. 4. Métis--Prairie Provinces--Biography.
I. Title. II. Series: Amazing stories (Canmore, Alta.)

FC3217.1.R53K54 2004   971.05'1'092   C2003-907431-5

An application for the trademark for Amazing Stories™
has been made and the registered trademark is pending.

Printed and bound in Canada by Friesens
2 4 6 8 9 7 5 3 1

Cover: Louis Riel, photographed in Montreal in 1868.
(Reproduced courtesy of the Glenbow Archives)

Contents

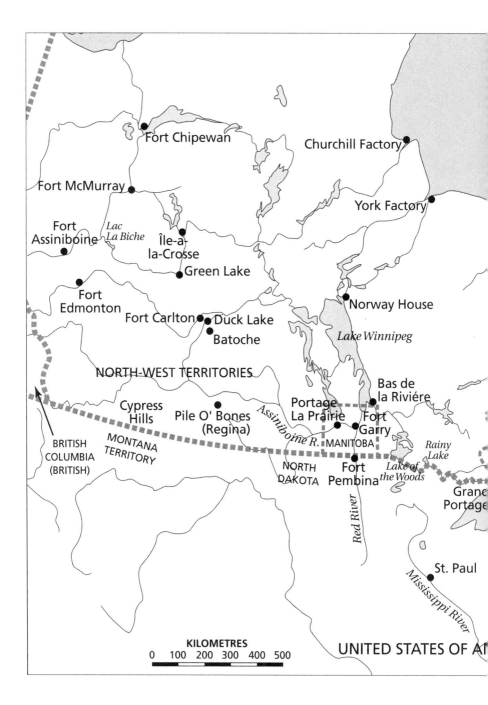

Fort Chipewan

Churchill Factory

Fort McMurray

York Factory

Fort
Assiniboine

*Lac
La Biche*

Île-a-
la-Crosse

Green Lake

Norway House

Fort
Edmonton

Fort Carlton Duck Lake

Batoche

Lake Winnipeg

NORTH-WEST TERRITORIES

Bas de
la Riviére

Cypress
Hills

Pile O' Bones
(Regina)

Assiniboine R.

Portage
La Prairie

Fort
Garry

BRITISH
COLUMBIA
(BRITISH)

MONTANA
TERRITORY

MANITOBA

*Rainy
Lake*

NORTH
DAKOTA

Fort
Pembina

*Lake of
the Woods*

Grand
Portage

Red River

St. Paul

Mississippi River

KILOMETRES

0 100 200 300 400 500

UNITED STATES OF A

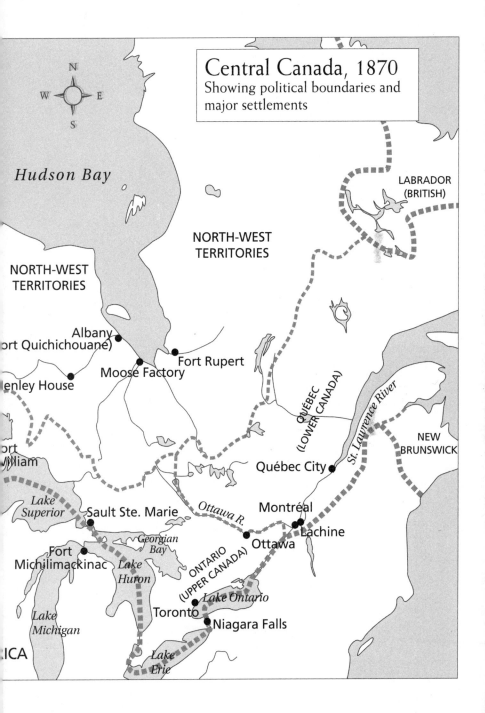

Central Canada, 1870
Showing political boundaries and major settlements

N
W E
S

Hudson Bay

NORTH-WEST
TERRITORIES

LABRADOR
(BRITISH)

NORTH-WEST
TERRITORIES

Albany
ort Quichichouane)

Fort Rupert

Moose Factory

enley House

QUÉBEC
(LOWER CANADA)

St. Lawrence River

NEW
BRUNSWICK

ort
illiam

Québec City

Lake
Superior

Sault Ste. Marie

Ottawa R.

Montréal

Lachine

Fort
Michilimackinac

Georgian
Bay

Lake
Huron

ONTARIO
(UPPER CANADA)

Ottawa

Lake
Michigan

Lake Ontario

Toronto

Niagara Falls

ICA

Lake
Erie

Prologue

Summer 1885

The audience was restless, waiting for the Prophet to speak. Many of them had travelled to Regina just for a glimpse of the great man. The building was crowded. Every last seat was full. A window had been thrown open, but there was no escaping the summer heat. The doors were kept bolted at all times.

A droning voice filled the air. It spoke of a great sin, and of possible redemption. Outside, a grasshopper droned in reply. There was no other sound save the odd restless cough and the scraping of chair legs on the floor.

The Prophet stood before them. He was close enough to reach out and touch. But no one dared try it. Many of them were on edge. His followers were fanatics. They might burst in at any minute and carry him away.

The time had come. Louis Riel, the Prophet, was ready to say his piece. He gripped the rail and leaned forward. He had waited a long time for this chance to speak of his mission. One group of men in particular caught his attention. He fixed them with his dark, piercing gaze. But their own eyes, when they looked back, were hostile or indifferent. Suddenly, he remembered. This wasn't a pulpit. It was a prisoner's box. And the men seated before him weren't his congregation. Riel stood accused of grand treason, and they were the jury...

Introduction

Today, when we look at the map of Canada, we see 10 provinces stretching across the continent. In the east, the cluster of Maritime provinces and the behemoths of Quebec and Ontario. Moving westward, aligned as straight as toy soldiers, are Manitoba, Saskatchewan, Alberta, and British Columbia. To the north, three vast territories stretch to the Arctic.

But at the close of the 19th century, this northern section of the continent did not look so neatly organized. Instead, it resembled a giant puzzle, slowly being fitted together. The land, once a series of British colonies, was making the slow journey towards nationhood. In the east lay the seats of power, Ontario and Quebec, then known as Upper and Lower Canada. To the west stretched a vast, untamed expanse known as the British North-West Territories. Larger than the whole of Europe and sparsely populated, this was the semi-mythical Wild West where bands of Native peoples hunted buffalo that swarmed over the grassy plains.

The Incredible Adventures of Louis Riel

The British government, in 1670, had granted a portion of this wilderness to the British fur-trading giant, the Hudson's Bay Company. This area, situated southwest of the Hudson Bay — in the present day province of Manitoba — was dubbed "Rupert's Land." The Company's employees, mostly of French and British origin, roamed the land, hunting, trapping, and trading in animal hides. Though most eventually returned to their European homes, many married Native women and settled down in their adopted homeland. The children of these unions became known as "Métis," after the French word for "mixed blood."

In 1812, 130 square kilometres of the southern portion of Rupert's Land was set aside for retired Company men and their families. Located at the junction of the Red and Assiniboine rivers — on the site of present day Winnipeg — the area became known as the Red River Settlement, district of Assiniboia.

By the mid 1850s, British power was on the wane in North America. While Canada struggled to establish a national identity, a new nation, the Métis, was trying to establish itself. In the British-run colony of Red River, trouble was brewing...

Chapter 1
The Making of a Rebel

hen Louis Riel left his family's home-stead in the summer of 1858, he was a youth of 13, raw but full of promise. He likely had mixed feelings about leaving Red River, the small Métis settlement in the heart of Rupert's Land. Few of his peers had dreamed of a life beyond the iso-lated settlement. Theirs was a limited existence in every way; illiteracy was the norm among them. If they were lucky, they picked up a few scraps of learning from the local priests and nuns before settling down to the traditional Métis way of life: farming in the summer, then hunting and trapping throughout the harsh prairie

winter. It was an arduous life, with no room for dreamers.

But Riel, a clever, introspective boy, had always known he wasn't cut out for this hardscrabble existence. Even as a child he had stood apart from his rough-and-tumble classmates. His parents, both devout Catholics, were fervently religious. Before they met, his father had briefly studied to be a priest, and his mother had wanted to enter a convent. They prayed that their children, all nine of them, would join religious orders when they grew up. They began to indoctrinate their first-born son early. The first words little Louis learned on his mother's knees were "Jésus, Marie, et Joseph." He never forgot to cross himself and say his prayers every night, before going to bed.

His parents also taught him obedience and self-control. Once, while he was at school in his parish of St. Boniface, a boy had challenged him to a fight following a schoolyard argument. The young Riel hesitated, then announced that he needed his mother's permission first. "If she says yes," he promised, "we will meet again!" Although he deferred to his parents, Riel was no coward, and never let others take advantage of him. He firmly believed in standing up for the underdog. As a schoolmate later observed, "Nothing irritated him as much as an abuse of strength against the weak." He was a compassionate boy who would give his lunch to children even poorer than he was, though it meant going hungry himself.

As he matured, his piety and studious nature served him well. When he reached his teens, he was chosen to study Latin under the guidance of the parish priest. Only three other boys from his school earned that honour. Latin would be his fourth language: besides his native French, he had a smattering of English and Cree. His teachers were thrilled by their find. Riel was unusually bright and eager to learn. With the proper training, they hoped, he might even become a priest.

The only suitable religious school, however, was a five-week journey away, in the Canadian province of Quebec. Riel's father, Louis Sr., worked odd jobs and could not afford the travel costs and tuition fees that the school would entail. With an ever-expanding brood to feed and clothe, it was often a struggle to make ends meet. But the local bishop, Monsignor Taché, had been watching the gifted young man. With the help of a wealthy patron, he arranged scholarships for young Riel and two other promising students. On June 1, 1858, the three boys, with a nun as a chaperone, set out by oxcart on the first leg of the 2400-kilometre journey to Quebec.

The Seminary

There were no roads through the empty wilderness between Rupert's Land and Canada, so the small party first headed south to the United States. At their first stop after crossing the border into Minnesota, Riel was briefly reunited with his father, who happened to be trading in the area. Father and son had always been close. They embraced tearfully when it was time to go their separate ways.

The boys continued their journey by cart, ferry, steamboat, and rail. As they travelled eastward, their fear and excitement mounted. There was little they could say to reassure one another. It wasn't just the very real threat of a Sioux attack that frightened them. Once they reached Quebec, they would all head off in different directions. Riel's friends were going to study at the seminaries in the small towns of Nicolet and St. Hyacinthe, but it was Riel who had landed the plum position. He would be studying at the prestigious College of Montreal in the heart of that cosmopolitan port city.

In September, just a month before his 14th birthday, Riel began his studies at the college. As he passed through its portals for the first time, he imagined he was entering a whole new world. The imposing stone building was a far cry from the rough log cabin he had called home. The young student was in awe. A "wonderful institution" was how he described the place in later years. His teachers, all priests, led a life of order and obedience, and they expected their students to follow suit. Riel quickly became used to the novelty of weekly baths, the bland diet of boiled beef and porridge, and the rigorous daily regimen of prayers and study. In some ways, life at the school was as restricted as life had been in the settlement. Riel and his schoolmates were allowed little outside distraction; even newspapers were banned. But Riel's new life wasn't all strictness and deprivation. The boys were allowed treats such as oranges — an unheard of luxury in Red River. Riel would always remember the first time he tasted the exotic fruit. The flavour was unforgettable, a sweet and sticky surprise.

The teenager was slow to adjust to his new life, and his grades suffered as a consequence. But once he settled in, he became enthralled by his studies — religion, philosophy, Latin, and other classical subjects. As the years went on he became an outstanding student, frequently at the top of his class. He developed an interest in poetry, and began writing fables in the style of the French master, La Fontaine. His family and friends in Red River were thrilled with his success. They had high hopes for this boy. He could be the first of their kind to become both a priest and a missionary — a position of status and influence in their eyes. Riel's future looked bright.

But a few months before he was due to take his final exams, that bright future suddenly faded. On a bleak winter's day in 1864, the 19-year-old learned that his beloved father had passed away. Riel wept like a child. The journey to the settlement was so arduous and expensive, he had been unable to return home since starting college. He had not seen his father since that day in June, six years before. Now, he was inconsolable. His father had been his hero and role model. Though he had experienced many failures in his life, Louis Riel Sr. had been an important political figure in Red River. Though he was a miller by trade, he had also been an activist and spokesman for the Métis free traders. In the troubled early days of the settlement, he had inspired his countrymen with his fiery speeches about Métis representation and protection of the French language in the face of British indifference.

Louis Riel inherited his father's fiery nature and his skill with words; he now inherited his father's responsibilities. On that fateful day, the sheltered seminary student became head of a large family. Despite his love for his mother and siblings, Riel decided not to return home to help provide for them. Though he remained at the college for a while, he gradually lost interest in his studies. His grades began to slide. In the depth of misery, he wrote long, mournful letters to his mother and composed sad poetry instead of studying.

In early 1865, he left college without receiving his degree. His aunt and uncle, the Lees, invited him to live with them in their village near Montreal. He had been a frequent guest of theirs in the past, during breaks from his studies; it was here that he met and fell in love with young Marie-Julie Guenon.

The girl's parents, neighbours of the Lees, disapproved of the burgeoning love affair between the two young people. Whether this was because Riel was Métis, or because he was unemployed, is unclear. In 19th century Canada, white society had a condescending attitude towards Native peoples and the Métis; it is likely Marie-Julie's parents considered the young suitor to be uncultured and socially inferior. Nothing could have been farther from the truth. Riel was now a well-educated, well-dressed young man with a pleasing appearance. He was tall, handsome, and debonair, and wore his dark hair fashionably long. And despite the disapproval of others, he had been raised to be proud of his heritage. His mother, Julie Lagimodière, was one of the first white women to live in the Red River Settlement, and proudly claimed that she was of aristocratic French stock. His father was of mixed French and Chipewyan blood — a true Métis.

In secret, Riel and Marie-Julie signed a marriage contract, a form of Victorian pre-nuptial agreement. In it, he renounced any claim to her very modest fortune. When Marie-Julie's parents discovered their plans, they were furious. The young lovers were forced to call off the wedding. It proved to be the end of their romance.

Although the love affair ended in heartbreak, it made Riel realize he was not meant for the celibate life of a priest. Disillusioned and unhappy, he set out to find a new vocation. He worked briefly in a law office, and toyed with the idea of becoming a merchant in the fur trade. Nothing came of these aspirations. His friends, meanwhile, began to grow concerned. Riel's ambitions had begun to sound like futile dreams. He claimed to a potential business partner that he had £1000 to invest. This was likely untrue; Riel was more poverty-stricken than ever before. During this time, an acquaintance wrote that Riel was a man of "no sense. He needs someone to guide him and follow him around..."

In the summer of 1866, only a week after the wedding was called off, Riel left Montreal. His family hoped he would return to Red River, but he wasn't yet ready. Perhaps he was ashamed. He knew he had disappointed them, and his entire community, by not completing his degree and entering the priesthood. His letters home, once so frequent, tapered off. Nothing much is known about his life during the next two years, except that he spent some time travelling around the United States, dabbling in different ventures. The letters he received from his family, meanwhile, were becoming increasingly frantic. Eventually, he could no longer ignore them. In July 1868, poor and unemployed, Louis Riel accepted the inevitable and returned to his family home in the Red River Settlement.

Tumult in Red River

Life on the prairies had always been hard. But when Riel returned to the West, the outlook was truly bleak. "Old Red River is going to the devil faster than ever," is how one settler summed up the situation. The Métis were a hardy people, used to the perils of farming. Living on the banks of a river, they were also prepared for the ever-present dangers of flooding. They had seen waterlogged crops rot in the fields, and watched helplessly as houses and farm equipment were swept away in the rising waters. In the past, they had often prayed for the rain to stop. In the hot, dry summer of 1868, they prayed for it to fall.

The drought brought unimagined hardships. The few crops the prairie soil yielded dried up in the sun-scorched fields. And what little remained of the potatoes and grain they planted was devoured by a terrifying infestation of grasshoppers. The insects swarmed through fields and along riverbanks. They found their way into houses, water barrels, food, and clothing. They carpeted the ground and crunched underfoot. "On the rivers they floated like scum," said one observer, "or were piled two feet deep on the banks, where they rotted and stunk like carrion." To the devout and superstitious Métis, the drought and infestation were disasters of biblical proportions. Perhaps, they conjectured, they were being punished for some unknown sin.

But they were also a resourceful people. Although the settlers had lost their crops, they were confident they would not starve. They were skilled horsemen and excellent marksmen. Every winter, they formed groups and hunted buffalo — the greatest prize of the prairies. The majestic animals were important not only for their meat, but for their hides: buffalo pelts were the backbone of the fur trade.

Hunting had always been a lucrative business for them. Though their Native relatives had long been their rivals in the hunt, there had always been enough buffalo for everyone. But in recent years, a new competitor had arrived on the plains: the sport hunter. Rich, privileged, and bored, these men came from Canada, the United States, and even Europe to bag their trophies. Big game was beginning to mean big profit. The massive animals, once so plentiful, were being over-hunted. The remaining herds now retreated westward. The Métis travelled farther and farther to find the herds, but came back with less meat and fewer hides.

Their desperation was mounting. Not only was the big game vanishing, there were no rabbits left to hunt and fish were scarce. The years of plenty had made them slightly complacent. It was not their way to save for leaner times. They had little money to buy staples, and few goods to give in trade. Though there was a famine relief program in place, it wasn't enough. A few meagre handouts of grain wouldn't keep them going for long.

The Riel family, though, were better off than many. Despite the loss of their crops, they still had cows and horses to trade or, if necessary, to eat. Riel, with his family's help, had enough to trade an ox, 100 pounds of beef, 22 aspen logs and a buffalo hide for a few plots of land surrounding his family's homestead. But for many others, starvation was frighteningly near. Some resorted to desperate acts. An unspeakable rumour circulated throughout the settlement: it was whispered that one family had been forced to kill their pet cat for meat.

As if the natural disasters were not enough, the settlers now had other worries. The political situation was again in turmoil. The settlement, though only a few decades old, had a tumultuous history. Originally it had been conceived as a retirement colony for employees of the Hudson's Bay Company, the British fur trading company that owned Rupert's Land. However, the residents of the settlement had other ideas: they perceived it as a Métis homeland.

The Métis had slowly begun to emerge as a nation. They had adopted a unique style of dress, a mixture of Native and European influences. The men wore Western-style clothing, ornamented with distinctive beaded knee bands and fringed sashes that dangled to their knees. On their feet they wore soft suede moccasins. The women were equally ornate, with their brightly coloured dresses and contrasting scarves knotted at the neck. The Métis had also developed a culture of their own. They composed and sang patriotic songs, praising the bravery of their men and the virtue of their women. They were a music-loving people, with a fiddle in every home. Though they remained British subjects, they began flying a flag of their own design alongside the Union Jack.

This growing nationalism had more than once led them to challenge the authority of the Company. The Métis valued their freedom and rights, and they were willing to fight to protect their way of life. Riel's father had been at the forefront of the agitations many years before, when the Métis had challenged the Company's monopoly on the fur trade. They had won that battle. But still, they were not a lawless people. An effective system of justice had evolved during the hunting seasons, when men were forced to cooperate, or perish. There was no jail. It was usually sufficient for the community to verbally shame a wrongdoer into changing his ways. The Métis had their own way of doing things.

But the Hudson's Bay Company, meanwhile, had decided to sell Rupert's Land, since its holdings in the region were no longer as profitable as they had once been. Two land-hungry nations had their eyes on it. For Canada, a westward expansion was only natural. The growing nation required more and more room for its expanding population. For many Canadians, it was a foregone conclusion: Rupert's Land, the wilderness to the west of their borders, would be theirs.

Down in the United States, however, there was an equally strong feeling that annexation was inevitable. The settlers in Rupert's Land relied on the U.S. for transport and communication: there were still no paved roads or railway tracks between the Red River area and Canada. Travellers journeyed on the routes that cut through the northern States — the same routes Louis Riel had taken 10 years earlier. The Métis, moreover, had other strong ties to the south, particularly to their neighbours and relatives in northern Montana. It was much more convenient for them to make a quick trip across the border to trade furs and other goods with the Americans than it was to make the five-week trek to Canada.

Unfortunately, fur trading with the U.S. was against the Company's laws. The practical Métis refused to believe that something so convenient could be illegal, and continued the practice. Before the decline of the buffalo herds, fur smuggling had been rampant — much to the dismay of the monopolistic Hudson's Bay Company. The desire for free trade with the U.S. was one of the reasons the Métis had chafed against the Company's rules and regulations. It is not surprising that many Métis favoured the American claim to the territory.

The key players in the sale of Rupert's Land — the British, the Canadians, and the Americans — were all eager to complete negotiations to their own advantage. But none of them gave any serious thought to what the Métis or the other settlers in the area wanted. These people, all 10,000 of them, were to be bought and sold along with the land they inhabited. In June 1869, The Hudson's Bay Company sold Rupert's Land to the Canadian government for a paltry £300,000.

The Canadian Invasion

The Métis were badly shaken. At no point had they been

consulted regarding the sale. And when a Canadian newspaper began touting the new acquisition as prime real estate, they became alarmed. The Métis, it was suggested, were nothing but a hapless bunch bent on destroying themselves. It would be easy to force them out of the country. Their land was ripe for the picking.

The Métis knew most white Canadians held them in low regard and felt their wants and needs were not worthy of serious consideration. They also knew that if an influx of white, Protestant, English-speaking people flooded their land, their entire culture could be lost. They feared that their rights would be trampled and that their farmland would be taken over by these "foreigners" from Canada. They might be left homeless, in an even more precarious situation than they already were.

The Canadians did little to dispel these fears. They moved in quickly during the summer of 1869, sending men to survey the land even before authority had been officially transferred to the new government. The Métis feared and distrusted the surveyors. They studied the area where they meant to build roads, which was acceptable. But they also came to look at Métis farmland, which was not. One thing was becoming clear: this was a time of crisis, and the people of Red River needed someone to lead them more desperately than ever.

Louis Riel's name must have immediately sprung

to their minds. Not only was he educated, intelligent, and eloquent, he was physically imposing, and capable of commanding a crowd. The people of Red River had naturally deferred to this man whose clothes, manners, and education were all far superior to their own. Now that they needed a strong leader, they turned to him. Despite his impressive demeanour, he was one of their own. His father had been a respected leader among them; it seemed that Louis Riel had literally been born to lead the Métis people.

His first move was hardly the act of a bloodthirsty rebel. It was a carefully thought-out letter to the editor of a French-Canadian newspaper, *Le Nouveau Monde*. Riel knew the people of Quebec were sympathetic to the Métis; they shared the same language and religion. He felt sure they would listen to him. In his letter, Riel defended the Métis character and chastised the paper for suggesting that Canadians could easily take over their land. It was a good first move: it gave a subtle warning that the Métis were not all backward folk, easily manipulated, and it gave Riel a little recognition as well. The next step would be a much more serious endeavour. It was time to rally the Métis and show the Canadian government the error of their ways.

In Defence of Liberty

Meeting in secret, Riel and his co-conspirators began to organize a movement against the Canadian takeover. Calling themselves the National Committee, they vowed to resist the efforts to take over their land. They insisted that they were still British subjects, not Canadian, and that in the absence of British rule the "natural, wise and just laws of the prairie" would prevail, not the imported laws of the Canadians. Four hundred Métis pledged to enforce the Committee's laws. They patrolled their territory, hunting rifles always by their sides. Their priests persuaded the men to keep violence to a minimum, but they were sensitive to Canadian insults and misdeeds and kept their fingers poised on their triggers.

Their first move was to put a rein on the Canadians' public works. Riel and his men approached a group of surveyors and, using thinly veiled threats, demanded they stop work. In October, they took a more serious step. William McDougall, the Canadian-appointed governor, had arrived at the border of Rupert's Land. He had intended to travel on to Fort Garry, the local seat of government in the heart of the settlement, but he was allowed to go no farther than the border.

This was not yet a revolution. The Métis greeted McDougall with roadblocks and a proclamation, not a volley of gunshot. The proclamation was formal and polite, but the meaning was clear. "The National Committee of the Métis of Red River orders William McDougall not to enter the Territory of the North West without special permission of the above-mentioned committee," it read. The arrogant Canadian official was outraged and was determined to defy the proclamation. He waited until November, then tried to enter the territory again. He got no more than 5 kilometres into the settlement before he was stopped and escorted back into Minnesota. Riel insisted that his men were breaking no laws. They were "simply acting in defence of their own liberty."

McDougall was flabbergasted. He had been completely unprepared for this turn of events. No one in Ottawa, the Canadian capital, had an inkling there would be any resistance to the transfer of land. The Métis needed some kind of leverage to convince the Canadian government they were in earnest. Because the Canadians had no contingency plans, Fort Garry was left understaffed and vulnerable to attack. The fort contained the Hudson's Bay stores, stacked with much-needed provisions. The rebels' next target was obvious.

Riel and 120 of his men walked slowly up the road towards the fort. They were in no hurry, and their weapons were carefully concealed under their coats. Clustered in small unthreatening groups, they strolled up to the governor's private entrance, past the sights of the unmanned cannons, and went through the doors, unchecked. When someone finally moved to stop them, Riel blandly informed him that they had come "to guard the fort." There was no further resistance. Fort Garry, and all that lay within, was theirs for the taking. Without a single shot being fired, the Métis had bested the Canadian usurpers.

The Canadians had proved to be both ineffectual and unwilling to negotiate. In Riel's mind, that left the Métis with only one choice: they must establish their own provisional government. Some residents of the settlement, particularly the English-speaking Métis, thought this was going too far. They had more in common with the Canadian "immigrants" and felt less threatened by the land transfer.

But Riel the emerging politician was able to persuade them to his point of view. To those who doubted him, he said scornfully, "Go, return peacefully to your farms!" He told them that if they did nothing, they would inevitably be trampled by the will of a foreign power. But those who would follow him, he proclaimed, would be free to shape their own destiny. It was a powerful message. On a cold winter night in December 1869, a barrage of gunfire and fireworks illuminated the dark sky. Louis Riel, the prodigal Métis son, was proclaimed president of the newly formed Provisional Government of Rupert's Land.

Chapter 2
Trial and Error

ohn A. Macdonald, the prime minister, showed a flicker of annoyance. Those western rebels, the Métis, were preventing the proposed expansion of Canada. They had arrested some of the newly arrived Canadian settlers and charged them with disturbing the peace. The hapless newcomers were now under lock and key.

Although the ousted British administrators had agreed to stay in the settlement until the Canadians took over, they had lost all influence under Riel's Provisional Government. It was left to the Canadian prime minister to act. Faced with so much resistance, he announced that he had cancelled the transfer — for the time being. "You must bridle those gentlemen," Macdonald ordered his underlings, "or they will be a continued source of disquiet to you."

Privately, he worried that the situation would not be remedied quickly. Part of his solution was to send ambassadors to Rupert's Land to assure the Métis they had nothing to fear from Canada. "The intentions of the Government," the ambassadors assured Riel's council, "are altogether those of peace and good will." They were not, however, authorized to negotiate with the Métis. Instead, they were instructed to placate the insurgents — and distribute bribes. One ambassador had secretly been supplied with a purse full of "corruption funds." The Métis were still suffering financial hardships caused by the drought; the bribes were a temptation. A few men secretly accepted the Canadians' money and defected from the cause. It was rumoured the ambassadors had even tried to buy off Riel.

Riel was a man of principle, but he was also a man of extremes. He was not interested in the ambassadors' bribes, or their platitudes. "We claim no half-rights," he told a cheering crowd, "but all the rights we are entitled to...and what is more, Gentlemen, we will get them!" Increasingly, though, he seemed to be speaking more for himself than for those he represented; some members of his council were becoming wary of his boldness. When he made the shocking proposal to bypass negotiations with Canada and demand immediate provincial status for Rupert's Land instead, some of his supporters turned against him. The plan was far too audacious for them. But Riel made it plain that there would be no turning back. "The devil take it; we must win!" he snapped. In his view, the dissenters were traitors. Such treachery, he implied, would not be tolerated.

Fort Garry, the former Hudson's Bay bastion, was now being used to incarcerate anyone who dared to oppose the rebels. The flag of the Provisional Government now flew proudly from its ramparts. Inside, three rooms had been set aside to form a makeshift prison. Jailing wrongdoers, however, did not sit well with the Métis. As a result, they ensured that conditions in the prison, while primitive, were not harsh. The prisoners were given pemmican — strips of dried buffalo meat — and water at mealtimes. Riel himself gave the Canadian captives newspapers so they could keep abreast of the political situation. And on Christmas Day, the prisoners were treated to a meal of roast beef and plum pudding. The Métis even organized a dance for them, and played their fiddles to raise their spirits. But the prisoners, naturally, longed for freedom. The jailers would have happily released them if they would agree to the only Métis demand: an oath of loyalty and promise of good behaviour. But the Canadians refused on principle. They planned to escape instead.

Flight from Fort Garry
Riel would never have guessed that his prisoners might attempt a jailbreak. Although the fort lacked security, there was a more daunting barrier outside the walls: the weather. To venture outside during a prairie winter without adequate clothing was to risk frostbite, hypothermia, even death. Only a fool would attempt it. But during the early months of 1870, a few of the bolder prisoners took the risk. They pried apart the decaying wooden casement of a window with a blunt knife and pried out the iron bars. One man cut his buffalo robe into strips and fashioned a crude rope out of it. He and the other prisoners then shimmied down the side of the building, and fled into the night.

Nine captives escaped. A few were recaptured, but some found refuge in the nearby settlement of Portage la Prairie, where other Canadian settlers were living. These men offered the fugitives food, shelter, and a sympathetic ear. They were outraged at the treatment their countrymen had received. The former prisoners and their sympathizers, a group of about 100, began to organize and arm themselves. They set out through the snow, intending to storm the fort and free the remaining prisoners.

Meanwhile, back at Fort Garry, Riel had persuaded all but one of the remaining prisoners to take the hated loyalty oath. Then, true to his word, he released them all — even the lone dissenter.

The news soon reached the would-be rescuers. Still angry, and determined to avenge the perceived injustice, they decided on a new target: Louis Riel. They had heard a rumour that he was staying with friends in Winnipeg, which was, at the time, just a small town near Fort Garry. Under cover of night, they crept up to the house and silently surrounded it in order to cut off all escape routes. At a signal, two of the men rushed up to the house and burst through the door, demanding the surrender of Riel. They were met with blank looks from the startled inhabitants. Louis Riel was not there. When the Canadians realized their mistake, they quickly backed down. They apologized to the wronged homeowners and started back home, chastened.

Rumours of War
The rebellion, up to this point, had been staged with remarkably little bloodshed. Though there was plenty of aggressive talk and righteous indignation on both sides, no one wanted to be the first to start an all-out war. The

peace was precarious, however. One incident left the adversaries teetering on the edge of armed conflict. In February 1870, a Métis named Norbert Parisien was seized by Canadian officials and accused of being a spy. He was armed, and fired off a few rounds in self-defence. A Canadian bystander was struck by a stray bullet, and fatally injured. In retaliation, his angry captors beat the man to death.

Riel was horrified. He hastily scribbled the Canadian officials a letter. He pointed out that no one wanted "horrible civil war" and reminded them how he had shown himself a man of honour, releasing all the Fort Garry prisoners unharmed. The Canadians were willing to be mollified. They agreed that this was nothing more than an unfortunate "accident." For the time being, both sides backed down.

But Riel was getting nervous. Talk had slowly turned from civil rights to civil war. The slack security around Fort Garry was tightened; 500 men now patrolled its grounds. The chances that this was to be a bloodless coup were becoming increasingly slim. Women and children were evacuated from the Fort Garry region and transported to a safe site, out of the reach of gunshot and cannon fire.

On February 19, Riel thought his worst fears were about to be realized. A scout reported that 50 men on horses and sleighs were weaving their way through the snowdrifts towards the Fort. The Métis took their positions on the ramparts. Rifles were loaded and cannons were at the ready. A Métis party, some on horseback, some on foot, went out to engage the enemy. They surrounded the advancing group and seized their weapons.

But it wasn't a war party, after all. It was the dispirited group of former prisoners and their supporters returning from Winnipeg to Portage La Prairie. Unfortunately for them, the route took them within a few kilometres of the fort. They insisted they were merely taking the quickest route back to their homes, but the Métis did not believe the story. The Canadians soon found themselves staring through the iron bars of the Fort Garry cells — some for a second time.

Riel had repeatedly asserted his desire to maintain the peace, but this new threat could not be ignored. The repeated offences of the Canadians had tried his patience. He decided that the ringleader of this counter-rebellion, Major Charles Boulton, would have to be punished — immediately. Boulton, who was one of the surveyors arrested and jailed in 1869, had become the leader of the Canadian prisoners by virtue of his military training. Just hours after being thrown into a cell, he was brought in front of a makeshift court and put on trial. It took only a few minutes to decide his fate.

"Prepare to die tomorrow at 12 o'clock," Riel told the shocked prisoner.

Fortunately, some of Riel's advisors intervened and persuaded him to show mercy. Riel went to Boulton's cell himself to tell the frightened man that the death sentence had been commuted. This act of mercy was a wise move. If Boulton had been executed, the Canadian military would have descended on Riel and his men in an instant.

The Thomas Scott Affair
This time, it would take more than a loyalty oath to free the prisoners. Riel was determined that Boulton and the rest of the anti-revolutionaries would not set foot from Fort Garry until his Provisional Government had been recognized by Canadian officials. The prisoners knew how Riel felt and were growing restless in their cells.

Boulton, despite his military training, was losing control over the other men. He was a weakling, they thought, because he did not make a show of strength against the Métis. The prisoners began looking to one of the other men for leadership instead.

Thomas Scott was an Irish-Canadian, a Protestant Orangeman who had come west to work on the new roads. He had a reputation as a brawler — he had once tried to throw his boss into the river following a dispute.

The others admired his toughness. Unlike Boulton, Scott never hid his contempt for the Métis. He was a big man who stood over six feet tall, and he didn't hesitate to use his size to intimidate the Métis. He taunted and threatened his captors at every turn.

Finally, Scott wore out the jailers' patience. He had influenced the other prisoners and they, too, had become unruly. The guards were losing control. When Scott threw a punch at the Captain of the Guard, they dragged him from his cell, fists at the ready. They meant to beat some sense into him. One of Riel's advisors, hearing the disruption, managed to intervene. The fair thing to do, it was decided, was to report Scott's misdeeds to Riel. Their leader would know how to handle the mutiny.

Riel met with the guards, who complained at length about their captive's behaviour. Scott was a bigot and a bully, they said. He had to be disciplined. Riel placated his men, then talked to Scott in his cell. Keeping his own anger in check, he used his most reasonable tone to admonish the man, and explain how his violent behaviour would work against him.

Scott did not respond in kind. He despised the Métis leader, and spoke to him in an insulting manner. In his view, the Métis were a "bunch of cowards," and Riel was the worst of them. The president was angered by this affront to his dignity. Though he had clashed with Major Boulton, they had spoken to each other as one gentleman to another. Scott, on the other hand, was a ruffian who would not listen to reason. The brash Scott was put in shackles. Once again, a court was convened. The Canadian road-worker was to be tried, Métis-style, for "insubordination."

On the evening of March 3, the court was called into session. Scott was present for only half of the proceedings and spent the rest of the time in his cell. He spoke little French, so had not understood much of what was said, anyway. Witness after witness was called. They testified that Scott had assaulted his guards, slandered the president, Louis Riel, and attempted to overthrow the Provisional Government. As in Boulton's case, the proceedings moved quickly. Scott was soon found guilty. Some Métis proposed that his sentence should be exile, but the majority was in favour of a more serious punishment. For his crimes, Scott was sentenced to die. He would face a firing squad at noon the next day.

When the sentence was relayed to Scott in his cell, he shook his head in stunned disbelief. "I can hardly think they dare do it," he said in bewilderment to George Young, the minister who had been sent to comfort him.

A painting depicting Louis Riel's execution of Thomas Scott.

At noon on March 4, 1870, a restless crowd gathered outside the fort, where the execution was going to take place. They were about to witness the Métis' first violent revolutionary act after months of disputes and skirmishes. Scott was still in a state of disbelief. "This is horrible!" he said to Reverend Young moments before he was led in front of the firing squad. "This is cold-blooded murder!" Many residents of the settlement agreed and begged Riel to reconsider. Their leader was adamant. He had relented with Boulton, but he would show no weakness this time. "We must make Canada respect us," he said stolidly. "If necessary, others will follow."

Scott's hands were bound behind his back. A blindfold was knotted at the back of his head. He could no longer see the glare of sun on snow, or the Métis riflemen aiming at him. Four shots rang out. The white ground turned crimson where he fell. Thomas Scott would trouble the Métis no more.

Riel expressed his satisfaction. He believed that this show of strength would result in respect and obedience from the dissenters. The remaining prisoners, certainly, were very subdued. "Better days will come," he said optimistically, "because nothing violent can last."

His optimism was short lived. At only 26 years of age, he had just made the worst mistake of his political career.

Chapter 3
The Mission

n mid-March, 1870, Louis Riel prepared himself for the inevitable changes the next few months would bring. The snow was melting and the air was sweeter. Many of the Métis farmers were starting to think more of planting their crops than of rebellion. Others had simply lost interest in the fight. A few of Riel's men had already defected, and he was worried that his ambitions would be shattered by dissention within his own ranks. It was time to bring everyone back into the fold.

Riel addressed the problem at a meeting of his council. He told them they should present a united front and remain "cordial and united" in the face of their differences. He also suggested, for the sake of the more conservative of his men, that their old employer The Hudson's Bay Company might be reinstated at some time in the future. Furthermore, he announced he would resign as president should a more democratically chosen governor be sent from Ottawa. His men cheered him wildly for his conciliatory stance.

Despite this, many began to have doubts about their leader. They saw Riel's self-assurance as arrogance. One particularly unilateral move proved they were right. A party of delegates had been organized to travel to Ottawa to plead the Métis case. They were to present their List of Rights, which included the preservation of their customs and equality of the French and English languages, as well as a demand for provincial status. The official documents they were going to present named the new province. It was to be called Assiniboia — or so they thought.

Assiniboia had been the traditional name of the district since the early days of the Hudson's Bay Company. Without consulting his council, Riel had secretly amended the document before the delegates took it to Ottawa. He changed Assiniboia to Manitoba, a Native word that means "the god that speaks." When Riel finally confessed to his ruse, his supporters were incensed. He was brought up in front of his own council to explain his actions. He didn't have much of a defence. The change, he protested, was "for the better." But it was too late for the council to do undo what had been done. The delegates were on their way to Ottawa, the altered document safely packed away. Manitoba it would be.

The controversy over Riel's tampering was the last thing on the delegates' minds when they arrived in Ottawa on April 11. They had a bigger problem: how would they get anyone in power to listen to them? They need not have worried. They received all the attention they had hoped for — and more. Within days of setting foot in the Canadian capital, they were arrested on a charge of aiding and abetting the murder of Thomas Scott.

The delegates were more indignant than afraid. They were certain the charges were without merit. Prime Minister John A. Macdonald had already promised an amnesty to everyone who had participated in the rebellion. Even though the amnesty had been offered before the execution of Thomas Scott, the Métis assumed it would cover this act. The incident had not, to their knowledge, caused much of an uproar in Canada.

But this was the age of the newspaper, the train, and the telegraph. News travelled slowly, but travel it did. Nearly two months after the execution, English

Canadians were beginning to rise up in anger over the death of one of their own. A heinous crime had been committed, they said. The public demanded retribution, and the delegates were the first to be punished. Luckily, the charges were dropped. The delegates were free to carry on with their negotiations.

In mid-May, the settlers in Red River received a telegram from Ottawa. "The Manitoba Act is sanctioned," it read. "It is satisfactory." Manitoba would soon be a province, and the Métis were to be accorded the rights of every Canadian citizen. Riel and the rebels had won. The Manitobans rejoiced and hailed their leader as a hero.

Uproar in Ontario
In English Canada, meanwhile, the propaganda machine began its work. The dormant anti-French sentiment in the hearts of Ontarians awoke with a vengeance. English Canadians, it was said, were suffering atrocities at the hands of the French-speaking Métis. Thomas Scott, it was rumoured, hadn't been killed outright by the firing squad. Riddled with bullets, but still alive, he had been thrown into his wooden coffin and left to die a prolonged and painful death. One protester claimed that the Métis had "robbed, imprisoned and murdered loyal Canadians whose only crime was

devotion to the old flag." These inflammatory statements had one purpose: they were a call to arms. Any Canadian with a scrap of patriotism in him would long to see Scott's death avenged.

The rumours became increasingly morbid and sensational. One man claimed to have a vial of Scott's blood; another, a piece of rope that supposedly bound the dead man's wrists. Posters with provocative messages were put up for all to see. "Shall French Rebels Rule Our Dominion?" one roared. Riel's name was uttered with disgust. Many of the rumours were spread at "indignation meetings" designed to stir up resentment towards the Métis.

Finally, the government was forced to take action to satisfy public opinion. Publicly, officials were still negotiating with the Métis. On July 15, 1870, Manitoba formally became Canada's fifth province. Secretly, they were withdrawing the promised amnesty and mustering an army to send to Red River. The armed force was said to be support for Manitoba's first lieutenant-governor, Sir A.G. Archibald. Riel, as he had promised, was willing to resign in his favour as soon as he arrived. However, the 800 Canadian volunteers included many men who had joined the troops specifically to avenge Scott's death. The troops arrived at the settlement weeks ahead of the governor. Riel, though satisfied that he had completed his mission, was now in mortal danger.

The Escape

On the morning of August 24, 1870, Riel was in his rooms at Fort Garry, preparing for Archibald's arrival, when a friend thundered up on horseback and told him of the government's real intentions. "For the love of God, clear out," the man cried. "The troops are only two miles from the city and you are going to be lynched!" In the distance, soldiers could be seen moving purposefully over the prairie landscape. Taking refuge at the house of the local bishop, the erstwhile leader told him, "No matter what happens now, the rights of the Métis are assured by the Manitoba Act." After saying his goodbyes to his mother, he left for the safety of Montana with two loyal companions. This farewell must have been more painful than his first departure from the settlement, 12 years earlier. This time, his future held little promise.

Their escape was fraught with obstacles. When the three awoke the morning after leaving Red River, they were dismayed to find their horses had disappeared. They had no choice but to continue the journey on foot. They walked for a while, but, fearful they were being pursued, decided on a faster mode of travel. They tore down a nearby fence and tied the posts together with strips of their own clothing. They launched the leaky craft and let the river carry them towards their destination. At some point, they abandoned the raft and resumed their trek on land. Riel, now wet and tired, lost a shoe in the confusion. The dignified former leader was forced to limp over the rough terrain, half-shod. Exhausted, filthy, and still in shock over their sudden change in fortunes, the fugitives finally reached the border, and safety.

From his haven in the States, Riel was able to secretly communicate with his men in Manitoba. He was angry and distressed by the reports that trickled back to him. His departure had left his homeland without a guiding hand. A spirit of lawlessness had descended on the usually law-abiding Métis. There was public drunkenness, fist fights, and disorder. The military had overrun the settlement. Instead of imposing order, they were intimidating the Métis. Since they had not captured Riel, they took out their frustration on his countrymen. There was news of verbal assaults, beatings, and worse. A member of Thomas Scott's firing squad was found murdered by "persons unknown." Another Métis who had taken part in Scott's trial was hunted down by the soldiers and pelted with rocks. His tormentors then caught him up and threw him in the river, where they left him to drown.

Riel could not admit that his role in Scott's execution

was the cause of all this turmoil. "It is not reasonable that an individual should be held responsible for an act of government," he protested. To add to his misery, Riel feared he was still being hunted. A private citizen had put forward a sizeable reward for his capture. He moved around constantly, fearful that "assassins" were on his trail.

Thankfully, the anarchy in Manitoba didn't last. The governor finally arrived and restored order. He was even willing to extend the hand of friendship to Riel. The spirit was such that a group of Métis drafted a letter asking Riel to return and run in the provincial elections. Riel declined. Although he expected the amnesty would be granted soon, it was still too great a risk to return to Manitoba.

Macdonald's Gift

After several months of self-imposed exile, Riel decided it was safe to return to Manitoba, even though the amnesty had not yet been granted. Not everyone agreed that this was a wise move. In Ontario, a $5000 bounty had been placed on his head. Many were keen to claim it. But by December 1871, he was quietly living in Red River again. One day, a group of armed men stormed his house. Riel had gone out, leaving his sister Marie by herself. The men ransacked his belongings and threatened the girl. Riel felt guilty that his family was taking the brunt of the anger he had caused. He realized his return had been premature.

Through an intermediary, Riel was offered a bribe of $1000 to leave Canada. This time, he accepted the offer: he needed the money to feed his family. John A. Macdonald was delighted. He believed he had bought himself peace of mind from that "redoubtable gentleman," as he called him. "Where is Riel?" asked the hypocritical prime minister. "God knows, I wish I could lay my hands on him."

Under the name Louis Bissonette, Riel made his way to Minnesota, and not a moment too soon. In Canada, feelings against him were stronger than ever. His opponents had even burned him in effigy on the streets of Winnipeg. Many would rejoice to see him dead. Despite the obvious danger, Riel longed to return to Manitoba — but as a free man. This running and hiding went against the grain. He knew his only chance at freedom was to obtain the amnesty. And Riel believed he had found the way to get the long promised pardon.

At the suggestion of a friend, Riel announced his intention to run in the federal elections. As a Member of the Canadian Parliament, he believed, he would have both immunity from prosecution and the political clout to fight for amnesty for himself and the other Métis rebels. In 1872, abandoning his pseudonym and disregarding the deal he had made with Macdonald, he returned to Manitoba and began to campaign openly.

It was an audacious plan. Only a man with Riel's vision and self-confidence — or arrogance — could carry it off. He was by now the most notorious man in Canada, and a criminal in the eyes of many. His opponent in the election actually challenged him to a duel! But he still had the support of many Métis, and that worried the men in Ottawa. His popularity among the Manitoba voters virtually guaranteed his victory.

At this point, the Canadian government knew they could not arrest Riel without causing further political turmoil. This time, they proposed a trade-off instead of a bribe. Riel was asked to back down and allow a prominent French-Canadian poet and statesman, Sir George-Etienne Cartier, to run in his place. Riel admired the older man. Years before, when he was still living in Montreal, he had hoped to get a job working in Cartier's law office. Out of respect for the other man, and hoping this might provide leverage for the elusive amnesty, Riel agreed to withdraw from the elections.

With Riel backing him, Cartier won easily. But the older man was in ill health. He died in May of 1873, without ever having taken his seat in Parliament. The position was once again open. Freedom was like a sweet

The Mission

fruit to Riel; he could almost taste it. Though his friends were convinced he would be arrested if he was lucky, and murdered if he wasn't, he could not pass up this opportunity. Riel ran for MP a second time. And to the dismay of his enemies, he won.

Louis Riel, MP
Louis Riel was hiding in a very undignified spot for someone who had just been elected, unopposed, as Member of Parliament for Provencher, Manitoba. He was huddled under a haystack, breathing in the dusty air. After months of grumbling from the Canadian public about the government's ineffectual dealings with the rebel, a warrant had finally been issued for his arrest.

But luck was with him once again. He was not at home when the officers came to serve the warrant. A well-timed word had tipped him off and he had made his way to this most unlikely hiding place. When the coast was clear, Riel brushed the dust off his clothes and warily made his way to the new railway station. There was now a railroad from Manitoba to Ontario, and he intended to use it. Afraid, but still determined, he boarded the train for Ottawa, and the Houses of Parliament.

This latest venture was a terrible strain; Riel's nerves were on edge. He was certain men were hiding around every corner, waiting to leap out at him. He knew he could be arrested, or even murdered, at any minute on the streets of Ottawa. It was more than likely the guards in the House would set on him as soon as he passed through those hallowed doors. With two friends by his side, he cautiously approached the imposing stone buildings on Parliament Hill. He longed to take his seat and fight for amnesty but, at the last minute, his courage failed him. He turned and fled. The newly elected MP made hasty preparations to leave the country and once more seek refuge in the United States.

Riel's old enemy John A. Macdonald was no longer prime minister. He had lost his position after a political scandal: his party had accepted campaign contributions from the company that subsequently won the right to build the transcontinental railway. But the change in leadership did not bode well for Riel. The new prime minister, Alexander Mackenzie, was an even worse enemy than Macdonald had been. Soon after arriving in the States, Riel found out that Mackenzie was planning to dissolve Parliament and call new elections. By this time, Riel had gathered his courage again. He decided to run for MP of Provencher for a third time.

His opponents, once again, did their best to keep him out of office by putting their best candidate forward. But the French-speaking Métis threw all their support behind Riel. He won for the second time. On a cold day in March of 1874, Riel returned to Ottawa and approached the Parliament buildings once more.

His fear of arrest had not abated. He knew he was in even more danger than before. Mackenzie had made it very clear that he was unwilling to negotiate with the Métis leader. He would be thrown in jail the minute he stepped foot on Parliament Hill. But to officially become an MP, he had to enter the Parliament buildings and sign the register. Riel realized that this wasn't the time to make a grand statement. He planned to slip in and out as unobtrusively as possible, in order to escape the attention of the guards.

His camouflage was an old college friend, Romuald Fiset, who now held the seat for Rimouski, Quebec. The two men entered Parliament through a side door, and approached the desk of the Clerk of the House. It was customary for an established member to swear in new members, and Riel wisely let Fiset do most of the talking. All he had to do was put his signature to paper, swear an oath to the Queen, and leave as quickly as possible. It wasn't until the men were hustling out the door that the clerk absently glanced down at the register and realized who the new MP was. He looked up in horror at the two departing figures. Riel caught his eye. He gave the clerk a gallant little bow and was gone. Nothing could be done to reverse the process. Louis Riel was now officially a Member of Parliament.

The entire House was in an uproar. Louis Riel had been ordered to take his seat in Parliament but had not complied. He was still in hiding, too afraid to take the next step. Indignant MPs complained that Riel was a wanted man, not a respected politician. Realizing his plan to fight for amnesty from inside the House was impossible for the time being, he again left the country.

Mackenzie made it clear that he disapproved of these antics. He icily indicated he thought granting Manitoba provincial status was a mistake. A vote was taken on the Riel question. Should the rebel MP be allowed to keep his seat or not? Every French Canadian Member voted to keep him in. Every English Member voted to expel him. Riel was cast out by 56 votes.

In the States, Riel spent his time working to gain support for the amnesty and worrying about his friends who had participated in the rebellion. Many of them were now under arrest. Another Métis leader, Ambroise Lepine, had been tried and condemned to death for his part in the Scott affair. The situation was becoming more and more desperate. Then, in 1875, Riel's prayers were answered. John A. Macdonald, the "vampire" as Riel called him, was once again prime minister. Macdonald was keen to settle the Riel situation once and for all. He announced that unconditional amnesty would be granted to all the Métis who had participated in the rebellion. The only exception would be the two ringleaders, Ambroise Lepine, whose death sentence had been commuted, and Louis Riel. Even these two men would be granted amnesty, but on one condition: they would be exiled from Canada for five years.

Relieved their persecution was over, most of the rebels settled down to a more peaceful life. Riel was happy for them. His banishment was painful, but he began to make a life for himself. He spoke passable English, and he was increasingly comfortable living in the United States. There was an added attraction to making his home south of the border. During the last two years, while he had been fighting for his place in Parliament, he had often sought refuge at the home of a priest, Father Fabien Barnabé, in the village of Keeseville near the Canadian border. The priest lived with his mother and his charming sister, Evalina. Riel was often to be found in the young lady's company. Though she was somewhat weak and sickly, Riel was drawn to her piety and sympathetic nature. They grew closer and closer, and it was understood that they would eventually marry. "You are one of the family," the priest said to him knowingly.

The Burning Cloud

Despite the comfort Evalina provided, Riel felt his life had fallen apart. At the age of 30, he was again homeless, poor, and unemployed. He frequently had to rely on the charity of friends to survive. The repeated setbacks in his political life had been a terrible strain. Even though he should have been safe under the terms of the amnesty, he still feared arrest or assassination. He made repeated pleas to the U.S. government for help in his personal cause, and even had an audience with President Ulysses A. Grant, but to no avail. It was hopeless. No one would come to his aid.

In this time of trouble, Riel increasingly turned to religion for comfort. Religion, he said, had always been "as much part of my nature as the air I breathe." But his devoutness had taken a strange turn. He began to hear voices and experience visions. Some of the apparitions were fairly benign. At one time, he said, the Virgin and child appeared before him while he was sitting at his desk writing a letter. Another episode he described was far more dramatic — and more troubling. While he was in Washington, he made a trek up a mountain and stopped to rest at the top. While there, "the same spirit who showed himself to Moses in the midst of the burning cloud appeared to me in the same manner…He said to me 'Rise up, Louis David Riel, you have a mission to fulfil'." Riel was dumbfounded. He believed he had received "divine notification" from God to again lead his people. The vision was the turning point in his life.

Though he told no one of his heavenly mission, those around him could hardly fail to see that something was going very wrong with him. His friends often found him on his knees, praying fervently. "God has begun to bless me," he raved. His piety was turning into a mania. He claimed he had the power to perform miracles and cure the sick. He told a prominent American politician that he could cure the man's paralysed leg with his healing powers. He was horribly embarrassed when the predicted cure failed to come about. It was another in a growing list of failures.

Riel continued to look to God for comfort. In church one day, he was overcome by a feeling of spiritual joy. It was so intense, he said, it was nearly painful. It was followed, just as suddenly, by a terrible depression. As he sat on the wooden pew, he began sobbing uncontrollably. He drew his handkerchief over his face, while the rest of the congregation sat in uncomfortable silence. Riel was clearly losing his grip on reality. His behaviour was becoming a public nuisance.

Though intense in his beliefs, Riel had always been polite and well mannered. Now he babbled and roared. He had been fastidious about his appearance. Now he tore at his clothes. No one could make him listen to reason. He was on a mission, after all. His friends the Barnabés were at their wit's ends. They were unable to subdue or console him. His uncontrollable weeping and shouting frightened them to the point that, in desperation, they wrote a frantic letter to Riel's uncle in Montreal, begging him to help.

John Lee could barely believe his eyes. This broken man could not be the self-confident young scholar he had known in Montreal. Riel was thin, weak, and barely rational. He clearly needed help. Exile or no exile, Lee decided to smuggle his nephew back into Canada to ensure he received proper care. It was a bold move; Riel was too far gone to be discreet. On the train home, he made bellowing sounds like a bull then shouted out "Don't laugh! I am a prophet! I am a prophet!" He had to be restrained from jumping from a moving carriage after he spotted a church from the window. Fortunately, no one recognized the Métis rebel. The passengers who witnessed his antics dismissed him as a madman.

For several months, the Lees tried to care for their troubled nephew. They hoped he would improve in a calm and loving environment, but his behaviour remained erratic and disturbing. At his most frenzied, he would rip off his clothing, scream and cry, and repeatedly assert, "I am a prophet!" to anyone who would listen. In one of his calm periods, his aunt and uncle escorted him to church. He leapt to his feet in the middle of Mass to challenge the priest. He was quickly ushered out of the building.

The Lees realized that Riel needed more help than they could give him. In March 1876, under the pseudonym Louis R. David, patient #565 entered the Hospital of St. Jean de Dieu in Montreal. The doctor who examined him feared he was suicidal; the patient feared he was about to be murdered. The nursing nuns, meanwhile, feared reprisals if they were found to be harbouring the infamous Métis leader. The Lees moved him elsewhere. Under the name Louis Larochelle, the freedom-loving Riel was incarcerated, for two long years, at the asylum at Beauport, Quebec.

The Asylum
In later years, Riel claimed that he had feigned his madness in order to hide from his persecutors. If this is so, he was a very skilled actor. The shouting and weeping continued. He would rip off his clothes, and send the guards on a merry chase as he ran up and down the hospital corridors, nude. He went on periodic hunger strikes. He had violent spells, and would fight with his keepers. He was paranoid, and accused his doctors of attempting to poison him. Moreover, he claimed that all

religious authority rightly stemmed from him. "I forbid you…to say or sing the holy mass," he commanded the hospital chaplain. He then broke into the hospital chapel and smashed the candles and altarpieces to pieces. His punishment was restraints and solitary confinement.

In his calmer periods, he would scribble in his journal for hours on end, outlining the mission God had entrusted him with. Riel was an intelligent, highly educated man, and his delusions were correspondingly complex. It is difficult to make sense of many of the visions and beliefs that he spouted at this time. Essentially, his political goals had become confused with his religious mania. He believed that a new era was dawning, where Manitoba would be the epicentre of religious life. Catholics from all over Europe would find a new home there. And they would worship a new pope. Riel himself would be "Prophet, Infallible Pontiff, and Priest-King." He took the middle name David, as revealed to him in the mountaintop vision. For a while, it looked as though Riel would never be himself again.

In 1878, however, the doctors considered Riel "more or less" cured. "He isn't pope any longer," said an observer. Riel was grateful for all the doctors had done for him. They had treated him "as charitably as any lunatic could be," he said. But he winced as they gave him some final words of advice. His doctors counselled him to forget the two things that agitated him the most: religion and politics. Peace and quiet and a hearty dose of fresh air was what he needed. This would mean the end of his public life, the end of everything he had struggled for. But he had no choice. It was either that, or madness. Louis Riel, the most notorious man in Canada, hung his head and agreed. He would move out west, to Montana, and become a farmer.

Chapter 4
American Rebel

valina Barnabé was worried. Unbe-
known to her mother and her brother,
she and Louis Riel were secretly
engaged to be married. But she feared that she lacked
the stamina to be a farmer's wife. Riel had already left for
Montana, and she was impatiently waiting for him to
send for her. She shared her concerns in her letters to
him. The words they exchanged were full of tenderness.
She sent him pressed flowers, "the emblem of my true
and sincere love." In return, Riel sent her a figurine of
Jesus, a symbol of their shared faith. In a poem to her, he
wrote, "I pray God will answer all my prayers/and bind
us soon in the sweetest union."

But Riel was gradually building a life that did not include Evalina. His plan to begin farming had fallen apart, and he was trying desperately to find other work. Life among the American-based Métis was a far cry from the dodges and intrigues of his former political life in Red River. It had its own set of challenges. Riel had never really had the chance to learn the typical Métis skills. He couldn't hunt or skin an animal. For all his superior airs, the other Métis must have pitied him. They gave him a gift of buffalo meat to help, but he didn't even know how to preserve it properly. It began to rot, so he had to throw it away.

Eventually, Riel found his feet. His language skills enabled him to find work as an interpreter. Though he was sometimes reduced to chopping and selling wood to make ends meet, his health was improving. Another incident made his life even more pleasant. He met a young Métis woman, more than 10 years his junior, who intrigued him. Like Evalina, Marguerite Monet was meek and adoring and suffered from poor health. Unlike her rival, she was illiterate. It was a strange match for the intellectual 37-year-old. But he was clearly in love and asked her to be his wife.

Riel never officially broke off his engagement to Evalina. He didn't have to. Though he had retired from public life, he was not out of the public eye. He was still of great interest to Canadian journalists. Evalina discovered he had married another woman by reading it in a newspaper. She was furious. Despite her meek nature, she bitterly accused him of "having destroyed forever the future of one who...loved you." Although he might have felt guilty about hurting her, he would not forsake his young wife. By this time, Marguerite was already pregnant with their first child.

Despite dabbling in local politics during the first few years of his exile, he had now had enough of Canadian politics. The quest for amnesty that had driven him for so long was no longer a priority. To those who asked, he now said, "I am not a murderer. I have not committed any crime. I have no need of a pardon." The official period of his exile was almost over, but it no longer mattered to him. In March 1883, Louis Riel renounced his British heritage and took the oath of U.S. citizenship. "I have chosen this country as my adopted land," he announced.

In Canada, however, the newly formed North West Mounted Police were not so sure that he had withdrawn from the Canadian political scene. It was in Riel's blood to lead and agitate for social reform. The police were taking note of his political activities south of the border. He was concerned with the state of the Métis in his adopted country and had tried to help them by agitating for land grants and by attempting to curtail the sale of whiskey. Riel rarely indulged in alcohol, apart from drinking wine at communion. He was aghast when he saw some drunken Métis women staggering down the road, having squandered their last few coins in a saloon while their children went hungry. He blamed whiskey for the Métis' poverty and lowly position in society. As always, he wanted to help. Riel was still influential enough to be appointed special deputy marshal in order to prosecute a man who had been selling alcohol to the Métis. But it was impossible to pursue the case. Although it was illegal to sell whiskey to Native peoples, it was perfectly legal to sell it to their relatives, the Métis. Nothing Riel did could change that fact; he felt he had failed in his efforts to protect his people.

Then another cause caught his attention. He decided to use his stature in the Métis community to influence the political scene. He moved among his people and urged them to vote Republican. Their candidate was "willing to protect the best interest of every American citizen regardless of race and color," he told them. He was so zealous that he was accused of selling his vote. The opposing party said he had bribed or coerced the Métis to vote his way and had even dragged ineligible Canadian Métis into the polling booths.

In his youth, Riel had used all his wiles to avoid

falling into the hands of the law. He was no longer as vigilant as he'd once been. For the first time, the former outlaw was arrested. His crime: election fraud. According to the local press, Riel was nothing but a "low scoundrel." Fortunately, the charges were soon dismissed due to lack of hard evidence. Riel, however, was crushed. His political ambitions had once again backfired.

"Indian Troubles"

But it was not this interest in American politics that worried the Canadian national police force. They were concerned he would become involved in the "Indian troubles" that had surfaced in the Canadian west. As with the Métis, poverty, alcohol abuse, and unresolved land claims plagued the Native peoples. The North West Mounted Police were justifiably worried about an uprising from the disgruntled tribes. Louis Riel knew of their discontent. He was as proud of the Chipewyan blood that ran through his veins as he was of the French. "I praise my ancestors," he exulted in one of his poems. He was willing to "fight the native people's righteous fight." The Métis often camped with the Native peoples of Montana. They weren't so different, after all. Riel began to dream of a more permanent union of the two groups. Perhaps a confederacy of Métis and Native peoples could be established. He could only imagine the might of their combined forces.

He had taken the first tentative steps towards such a union in 1879. Secretly travelling north across the border, he approached Red Stone, chief of the Assiniboine. He drew up a document asserting that he, Louis Riel, was the "true and rightful chief" of the Métis and Native peoples. He said that if they threw their support behind him, he would restore their land to them. Both men signed the document in red ink — or possibly blood. But the local North West Mounted Police superintendent heard of the conspiracy. He intervened and persuaded Red Stone to withdraw his support. The chief burned the document and sent word to Riel that the treaty was nullified.

Undeterred, Riel next approached the local Blackfoot, Cree, and Sioux tribes. Though some of their warriors were eager to do battle with the Mounted Police, their leaders, Crowfoot, Big Bear, and Sitting Bull, were hesitant. Big Bear had long been thinking about the idea of a Native confederacy, but he doubted Riel was the man to lead them. Riel simply did not have the reputation among them that he did with the Métis. The chiefs refused to accept him as their leader. Riel's dream of a Native/Métis confederacy slowly faded away.

A formal portrait of Louis Riel taken around 1879

Settling Down

Riel was starting to realize that involvement in politics would bring him nothing but trouble. He was tired of being treated as a "public nuisance" because of his beliefs. After several years of marriage, he and Marguerite had two young children, Jean and Marie Angelique. Riel doted on the youngsters. His new responsibilities led to a new stability. It was time to settle down to a life without politics.

He took a position as a schoolteacher at the nearby Jesuit mission, his first real full-time job. The great leader of men now taught Métis children the basics — reading, writing, and arithmetic. He was also responsible for their religious instruction. Once, this would have set off a wild-eyed ranting and raving. But the madness that had gripped him so violently no longer had a hold on him. He still had a mystical side, however. On one occasion, he claimed his long-dead father appeared before him and offered him his blessing. But these visions were milder than they used to be. Comforting, even.

Riel no longer had the time to be a prophet. He often worked 14-hour days, seven days a week. The gruelling schedule and the monotony began to tell on him. He looked for other employment, but nothing was available. "My enemies have trapped me beneath their blows," he groaned, "and I cannot escape." He could not forget that he had once been destined for greatness. Nearing 40, Riel resigned himself to a life of poverty and obscurity.

The Men From Saskatchewan

It was in this mood of quiet desperation that the four men found him. On a June morning in 1884, they rode to the church where Riel was attending mass. They called him from his prayers to discuss important business. They identified themselves as Gabriel Dumont, Michel Dumas, James Isbister, and Moïse Ouellette. They were Métis from northwest Canada. They had travelled hundreds of kilometres down to Montana, specifically to confer with him.

There was barely room for them all as they sat in his tiny, cramped cabin, quietly talking in French. As he listened to the four men, Riel must have been haunted by a sense of déjà vu. The tale they told was chillingly familiar. The Métis of Saskatchewan and the Northwest, they said, were facing the same problems that had troubled the Manitobans 15 years before. The buffalo had been hunted to the brink of extinction, and bad weather had decimated their crops. The poorest of the Métis were faced with the prospect of starvation. They feared that their land would be forcibly taken from them as well.

With Saskatchewan not yet part of Confederation, their supposed leaders in Ottawa remained indifferent to their plight. Both the French and English-speaking Métis were united in their anger. All they wanted were the same rights that had been granted to the Manitoba Métis. But it was not just the extinction of their own people that they feared. Their relatives, the Native peoples of the region, were also suffering. "They are our relatives," Dumont later said of the Canadian tribes. "When they are starving they come to us for relief, and we have to feed them. The Government is not doing right by them."

Riel understood. "The importance of the Indian causes are far above all other interests," he said. Something, they agreed, had to be done.

The Happiest Day

His contacts among the Red River Métis had kept him apprised of the situation in the north, but the delegates' tale stirred his emotions anew. His excitement must have mounted as the four men let their tale unfold. They were not there to complain, or even ask for his advice. They told him they needed someone with experience to present their grievances to Ottawa. They asked him to be their leader.

Riel looked at his grim surroundings. A few books, a few mementoes, and a few sticks of furniture. This was all he possessed. He did not even own the tiny house they were crammed into. His guests had been taken aback when they saw how the former rebel leader lived.

They told him there was more than enough room in their carts for him, Marguerite, their children, and all their meagre belongings. If, that is, he was willing to accept their proposition.

Riel could barely contain his excitement. This was one of the happiest days of his life. But he didn't want to appear too eager. He asked for one day to think over their proposition. But, secretly, he had already made up his mind. He would say yes to the delegates' proposal, and goodbye to the American dream.

Chapter 5
Western Hero

iel and his party arrived at Fish Creek, Saskatchewan, a few days later. This time, Riel did not have to fear that setting foot on Canadian soil would mean an encounter with men who wanted to see him hang. His period of exile was over, and this group of people was thrilled to receive him. Fifty wagonloads of well-wishers came to meet him. They greeted him with wild cheers and outbursts of patriotic song. They had forgotten the grief he had caused, and remembered only his heroism. Some hot-headed admirers fired gunshots into the air. Riel was touched by the outpouring of warmth and respect.

"Fifteen years ago," he told them, "I gave my heart to my nation, and I am ready to give it again."

Riel made the town of Batoche his home base, but he was acclaimed wherever he went. A banquet was held in his honour. His speeches were greeted with cheers and applause. People hung on his every word. At first, he never mentioned the word rebellion. Instead he preached unity and moderation. He couldn't believe how the tide had turned. Mindful of how the English had been the first to turn against him all those years ago, he had to be persuaded to appear in front of them. He had nothing to fear. Everyone, even the white settlers, had a grievance against the government. They were all on his side.

An Ally and a Friend

Gabriel Dumont became a great ally and a great friend to Riel. According to folklore, he had met Louis Riel many years before, at the time of the troubles in Manitoba. It was said that Dumont had approached Riel with an offer of his support, and an army of 500 men. Whether or not the story is true, Dumont was clearly a man to be reckoned with. Tough and taciturn, he had grown up a nomad, in the traditional Métis way. By age 25, he was the leader of the annual buffalo hunt. His skill with firearms and with bow and arrow was legendary.

Gabriel Dumont

It was rumoured that he could shoot a duck in the head from 100 paces.

Physically, the two men could not have been more different. Riel was tall, elegant, and mild-mannered; Dumont was stocky with a threatening demeanour. Riel was educated and a skilled orator. Dumont, like many of the Métis, was illiterate. But Dumont was no fool. He spoke six Native languages, in addition to his first language, French, and was a canny businessman. He ran the local ferry, and kept a store and a pool hall. A founding member of the local council, he had helped bring law and order to the northwest. To his credit, he never allowed his good fortune to become a source of jealousy among the poorer Métis. In times of trouble, he gave gifts of buffalo meat to those less fortunate than himself. Through his actions and words, he was more than able to command the respect and admiration of his people.

Initially, Dumont had seemed threatened by Riel's popularity. To a comrade, he had grumbled, "We need him here as our political leader. In other matters I am the chief here." But his initial distrust soon gave way to a kind of hero-worship. Dumont, though he was several years older than Riel, would defer to the younger man even when he disagreed with him. Riel was accomplishing what no one had believed possible: he was truly uniting the people. Under his direction, a national association of the Métis was formed. It was called the Union Métisse St. Joseph, named for their patron saint. "Now we are established as a nation," said Riel triumphantly.

A Dangerous Man

One segment of the population, however, had not been won over. The local clergy were slow to publicly throw their support behind Riel. Privately, they feared him. They saw him as a troublemaker, a "dangerous man" who would lead their flock astray. Riel was stunned. To him, priests were leaders among men. They had stood by his side when he had fought for Manitoba's provincial status. He had fully expected their support.

But there was a grain of truth behind the priests' fears. There were hints that Riel's old madness was returning. He claimed once again that he was on a heavenly mission. He was now "Prophet of the New World." People were willing to do anything he told them to do. The priests saw with fear that the Métis didn't just admire Riel, they were actually beginning to worship him. They were turning away from the church; their souls were in danger.

Aside from his inspirational speeches and prophetic claims, Riel was working on more practical methods of securing the Métis' rights. He sent a carefully crafted petition to Ottawa. The Métis wanted a decision on their land claims, and some form of financial compensation, as well. In reply to their demands, the government said they would, at some point in the future, address the Métis' problems. For now, they would have to be content with a census.

Riel was more than a little disappointed. His motivations were not entirely selfless. He believed that he, too, was due some compensation for all he'd been through. The government's telegram had not even mentioned him by name. However, Ottawa had not been above trying to buy his silence. A position on the Council of the North-West Territories was offered to him, with the further temptation of a salary of $1000 per year. Despite his poverty and dissatisfaction with his lot, Riel refused. "Do you think I would dirty my name by accepting an appointment like that?" he demanded. Both Riel and the Métis were becoming increasingly dissatisfied with the government's apathetic response to their troubles. It was time to take a different tack.

At a church meeting that fall, Riel announced that there was nothing more he could do. He told them he had never intended to spend more than a couple of months with them; his time was up. He was preparing to move back to the U.S. The crowd erupted at his words. An old-timer, speaking on behalf of the people, cried out, "If you leave, nephew, we will go with you." As one, they begged him to stay on and continue their fight. Riel looked out at the sea of faces. Were they ready to take the next step? "But the consequences?" he asked hesitantly. "We will accept them!" the people cried.

The North-West Rebellion Erupts
It was an end to the talk of peace and conciliation. Now

was the time for the Métis to "bare their teeth" and show Ottawa their wrath, Riel roared to the crowd. The Métis were no weaklings. The government would regret trying to push them around. "I have only to lift my finger," he shouted, "and you will see a vast multitude of nations rushing here who are only awaiting the signal on my part!"

Though no one was willing to openly defy Riel, some Métis were secretly reluctant to go along with his plans. One of Riel's kin, Charles Nolin, was among the doubters. It was hard to say, from one day to the next, if Riel and Nolin were allies or enemies. They had frequently clashed during the Manitoba rebellion. At one time, Riel had nearly had him arrested. But Nolin had been the first to open his home to the Riels on their arrival in Saskatchewan. Riel never knew if he could trust the man.

When Riel approached him, asking for his support in the event of an armed rebellion, Nolin hesitated. He was reluctant to refuse his increasingly powerful kinsman. Instead, he suggested the Métis observe a novena, nine days of reflection and prayer, before committing themselves to any serious action. Riel allowed himself to be swayed. They would see what answers their prayers would bring.

On the fifth day of the novena, one of the priests, Father Fourmond, decided he'd had enough of Riel and his talk. It was time to nip any signs of rebellion in the bud. During mass, he made an announcement. He coldly informed the congregation that any revolutionary acts would be punished by the church. The sacraments, their link to God, would be denied them; they were risking eternal damnation. The people had a choice: inaction or the fires of Hell. It was a very serious threat. It was also a serious blunder. The priest had misread his flock's feeling. Riel leaped to his feet at the challenge. The people weren't interested in the lies coming from this "pulpit of falsehood," he exclaimed. It was time for the Métis to defend "their most sacred rights" by any means necessary. After the service, Riel urged the people to join him on March 19, the final day of the novena, and to bring along their rifles. "The time has come," he proclaimed, "to rule this country or perish in the attempt!"

But on March 18, 1885, one day before the deadline, Riel was informed that a company of North West Mounted Police, 500 men strong, was about to descend on the rebels. It was an empty rumour, but it galvanized the Métis. The time had come to take action. Riel hastily assembled a group of armed supporters. They cornered a group of government officials, including the local Indian Agent, and took them captive. The prisoners would be used as leverage to force the Canadian government into negotiations.

But this uprising was not only against unjust rule by the government. It was against the rule of the Catholic Church, too. Taking their prisoners with them, the rebels made their way to a local church. When the priest refused to allow the building to be used as a rebel meeting-place, Riel pushed him aside. He would not let anyone to stand in his way. For many years after the event, people spoke of the sacrilegious scene that played out in the church aisles. "Who has brought me here?" Riel asked as he approached the altar. "The Lord God," he answered himself. "Who speaks through my mouth when I speak to you?" the prophet demanded. "It's God!" he replied. Then he encouraged his men to recreate the biblical scene of Jesus' triumphant entry into Jerusalem. His followers danced about the church, while Riel, exultant, sang to them. "Rome has fallen!" he cried out.

The priest, meanwhile, nearly choked on his rage. He accused Riel of being a heretic. The Prophet was unrepentant. He had a direct link to God. He would no longer defer to these false leaders. "Priests," he asserted, "are not religion."

After this strange ritual, Riel and his men descended on a local general store, Walters and Baker. Stepping through the door, Riel simply announced, "Mr. Walters, it has commenced." There was no need for further explanations. He commanded his men to take the guns and ammunition they needed, despite the shopkeeper's protests. Riel assured the man that once the rebellion was over and the Métis had triumphed over their oppressors, he would be recompensed for his losses. Then the shopkeeper was taken prisoner. Even local clergymen who continued to defy Riel were later imprisoned.

The Exovedate

The ninth and final day of the novena came and went. The hoped-for peace was not to be. The rebels had cut most of the telegraph lines, severing one of their few means of communication with the outside world. They were armed, and watchful. But their actions were not all destructive. A provisional government was formed, called the Exovedate, a latinate term signifying "those picked from the flock." Gabriel Dumont was named "Adjutant-General." Riel initially declined any formal role in the new Government. As "God's mouthpiece," he felt he was above such worldly positions.

Now the Exovedate, not some foreign power, would decide matters of policy. The Métis no longer answered to a "corrupt government" in Ottawa or a "false pope" in Rome. Under their new order, and under Riel's guidance, they renamed the days of the week to remove their pagan association. Monday would be named after Christ, Tuesday after Mary, and so on. These actions shocked the orthodox Catholics among the Métis. Riel and the Exovedate soon lost supporters. In retaliation, the leaders arrested some of the Métis who preached pacifism. Among the pacifists was Charles Nolin, Riel's own cousin.

The next step, Riel decided, would be to take over nearby Fort Carlton and demand the surrender of Superintendent Crozier of the North West Mounted Police. The Superintendent angrily refused to surrender. Riel weakly insisted that this was merely a "demonstration," not a rebellion. But later, when called upon to show reason, he could no longer contain himself. There would be a "war of extermination" if the Métis' demands weren't met. "Blood, blood, we want blood!" he ranted.

This violent attitude did not sit well with the English Métis. Most had now withdrawn their support. They were not convinced that he was the holy emissary he claimed to be. After a series of meetings, they decided to formally protest his rebellious actions. In an ironic twist, the man they choose to present their objections was named Thomas Scott. He informed Riel that they wished to remain neutral. But, in Riel's eyes, there was no room left for neutrality. "A strong union between the French and English halfbreeds is the only guarantee that there will be no bloodshed," he protested. But it was too late. Bloodshed, by this time, was almost inevitable.

Incident at Duck Lake

In late March 1885, the rebellion began in earnest. It started with a chance encounter. While Superintendent Crozier bided his time at Fort Carlton, awaiting his backup of 100 men, he sent a couple of his subordinates on horse and sleigh down to the store at Duck Lake to buy flour and other provisions. There they encountered a group of Métis who had just finished plundering the store for supplies. The two sides naturally clashed. Shouts and insults were hurled, though the violence did not go beyond pushing and shoving. One gun went off by accident, but no one was injured. But the police would not tolerate the insult to their honour. They turned back to the fort to complain to their superior. Before long, an armed group, including some volunteers from Prince Albert, set out on the 22 kilometre ride to Duck Lake to discipline the unruly rebels.

But the Mounties were not the only ones who would not tolerate insults. Sometime in the early afternoon, Louis Riel rode to Duck Lake with a troop of Métis soldiers and Native supporters from the Beardy and One Arrow reserves. Their numbers stood at nearly 300 men. Gabriel Dumont, who had organized the raid on the Duck Lake store, was waiting for them.

Though Riel was in favour of meeting the enemy face-on, Dumont counselled an ambush. They would use their wits, not brute force. They would fight the police force using the methods honed during the annual buffalo hunt. The Métis found cover in a log cabin on one side of the road, and in a wooded ditch on the other. Their marksmen cocked their pistols. Then they settled down to wait. Soon, the cry went up from the Métis scout. "Here come the police!"

The Mounties knew they were outnumbered, and paused to consider their options. They set up a barricade made up of 20 sleighs and readied their portable cannon. Both sides waited and hoped conflict could be avoided. The Métis sent over Gabriel Dumont's brother Isidore and a Native representative, Aseeweyin, to parley. The discussions did not go well. "Where are you going with so many guns, grandson?" taunted Aseeweyin, and made a grab for the interpreter's rifle. At that point, all semblance of civility vanished. Isidore and Aseeweyin bolted. With a shout, Crozier ordered his men to open fire on the Métis. Riel, unarmed but holding high a crucifix, shouted his own command. "Fire in the name of God the Father almighty!" he thundered. "Fire in the name of God the son! Fire in the name of God the Holy Spirit!" For the next 30 minutes, shots resounded throughout Duck Lake.

Though the police were better equipped than the Métis and Native warriors, they were still at a disadvantage. They were outnumbered roughly three to one. The Métis' superior knowledge of the local terrain gave them another edge. Realizing they could not beat the rebels, the Mounties began to retreat. Gabriel Dumont was in favour of giving chase and fighting. Riel, faced with the reality of warfare, begged him not to. There had already been too much bloodshed for his liking. The police had suffered 12 casualties; the Métis had lost five men. Isidore Dumont, who had acted as negotiator, had been one of the first to fall. Superintendent Crozier was wounded, and Gabriel Dumont narrowly escaped death when a bullet grazed his head. But Louis Riel was miraculously unharmed.

The police stayed long enough to gather up their dead, then retreated north to Prince Albert. Whether by accident or design, they set fire to Fort Carlton as they departed. The bodies of the militiamen were left to freeze in the snow. It was a clear victory for the Métis. Riel turned to his men and exclaimed, "Hurrah for Gabriel Dumont! Thank God who gave you so valiant a leader." He spent the rest of the day on his knees, praying for the souls of the dead.

With Fort Carlton in ashes, the Métis returned to Batoche. They were given an enthusiastic, almost reverential, reception. The Métis' victory and their leader's triumphant demeanour in battle had swayed the last of the French-speaking doubters. In a meeting of the Exovedate, the Métis adopted a new resolution: Louis Riel was officially a prophet of God.

The move against the Mounties was the last straw for many. The English-speaking whites and Métis now loudly opposed Riel. Even his cousin, Charles Nolin, who the Métis had freed in exchange for a promise of loyalty, had deserted and turned himself in to the North West Mounted Police. Though the Mounties had issued a proclamation stating that any Métis who peacefully surrendered would be protected, they opted to detain Nolin until the end of the rebellion.

Despite this loss of support, Riel thought he could muster more men from another source. "I hear the voice of the Indian," he said feverishly. "He comes to join me...He is in the mood for war." The Native peoples of the region, led by Poundmaker and Big Bear, were stirred up by the Métis' victory. They took up their rifles and began looting stores, and attacking whites. Riel gave them his blessing. "Rise: face the enemy...and come to us," he wrote to them. But despite his entreaties, the majority did not join forces with the Métis.

Even before the Duck Lake incident, the Canadian government had been mustering troops to subdue the Métis and Native insurgents. Feelings against the rebels ran high in Canada; volunteers from all over the country were quick to join up. They moved in two formations. Under the leadership of Major-General Frederick Middleton, 800 soldiers clad in blood-red uniforms began their march across the plains towards Batoche. Meanwhile, troops led by Major-General T.B. Strange, aimed to crush the Cree leader Big Bear. The two forces then planned to merge and overcome Poundmaker and his followers. In total, an estimated 8000 Canadian soldiers were to converge on the North-West Territories. Riel claimed that the "Spirit of God" was keeping him informed about the enemy's movements. In his journal, he inscribed the words, "I have seen the giant — he is coming, he is hideous. He is Goliath."

But Riel's confidence in God and himself remained unshaken. "I could go on the battlefield alone," he boasted. By this time, he was almost alone. Though he retained a core of true believers, only loyalty and pride kept most of the Métis from leaving Riel and his rebellion. They knew they would be crushed by the giant's fist and were reluctant to fight. But not Gabriel Dumont. He felt the Métis had to strike, and quickly.

Dumont outlined his plan. They would stage a series of guerrilla attacks on the Canadians. They would blow up bridges and train tracks, cutting off the military's supplies. Then they would creep out and attack the enemy camp at odd hours, harassing them and preventing them from sleeping. This way, the Métis might have a slight advantage. The Canadians, indeed, were afraid of such ambushes. But Riel insisted on a period of "fasting, prayer and mortification" before they took any action. And then, as before, he insisted that they would conduct a gentlemanly war. There would be no guerrilla attacks. The two sides must meet face to face.

Though he was dubious of Riel's abilities as a military strategist, Dumont, as usual, deferred to his wishes. "I had confidence in his faith and his prayers, and that God would listen to him," he later explained. He kept silent while Riel waited for the signal from God to fight. Finally, Dumont insisted they act. It was now or never. Riel gave in to the man he called "Uncle Gabriel" out of fondness and respect. And so Gabriel Dumont and his Métis army made for Fish Creek, just south of Batoche, where one year earlier a cheering crowd had greeted Louis Riel and his family.

Finally, on a cold, rainy day in April, the Métis prepared to face their opponents. Riel consoled himself by murmuring the words of the rosary. He prayed for God to crush his enemies; the Métis needed a miracle. Only a few Cree, Sioux, and Salteaux supporters, loyal to the Métis by blood and by treaty, had come to stand by Riel and his small band. The Métis of other regions were noticeably absent. They were unwilling to bring the wrath of the Canadian army down on themselves.

When Riel and Dumont set out from Batoche, they had only 200 Métis soldiers and a few dozen of their Native supporters behind them. The men, from the Métis farmer in homespun clothes, to the Teton Sioux in fringed and feathered battle dress, moved as quickly and unobtrusively as they could, their moccasins and horse's hooves sticking in the mud.

The small, motley army had not gone far when they received a message that Batoche was going to be attacked. Riel turned back with 25 foot soldiers and 25 horsemen to defend the women and children. During the confusion, more men deserted. Gabriel Dumont was now left with roughly 130 soldiers. Though worried by the dwindling numbers, Dumont was secretly relieved when Riel rode off. They could make better time without the distraction of his constant praying.

Knowing the Canadians were not far away, Dumont and his men fortified themselves with an early-morning feast of grilled bull's meat. With Riel gone, they could revert to their plans for an ambush. They hunkered down in brush and ravine and waited for the sound of marching footsteps. But a Canadian scout had spotted them. They had lost the element of surprise. Dumont, his blood boiling, charged after the scout and almost rode straight into the Canadians' advance guard. He quickly doubled back to his hiding place as the first shots rang out. One of the Natives, his face painted for battle, fell in a hail of bullets. He was the first of many casualties. Dumont, hoping to inspire his men with his bravery, galloped this way and that, shooting at every red uniform with his trusty rifle "Le Petit," or "the little one." The Canadians were so dazzled by this display, they estimated they were facing a force of 300 men.

But Dumont's soldiers were not inspired; they were afraid. Many panicked and ran. By mid-afternoon, Dumont had fewer than 50 men. To make matters worse, 55 horses, so essential to Métis warfare, had been killed. The general was desperate. He was even losing confidence in his capabilities. His head wound had become infected and he was having trouble thinking clearly. But at last, to his great relief, reinforcements arrived. His brother Edward had diverted 80 men on horseback from Batoche to help him.

Riel, meanwhile, had arrived in Batoche. But the threatened attack never came. With the sounds of battle ringing in the distance, he called out to the townspeople to gather around him. Kneeling, and stretching his arms out to form a cross, he began to pray for victory. The crowd prayed with him. When Riel's arms began to tire, two men rushed forward to hold them up. He stayed that way, a living crucifix, until he slumped forward from exhaustion.

On the battlefield, Middleton's men, though not defeated, decided to pull back for the time being. Many people, including Gabriel Dumont, credited their victory of that day to Riel's fervent prayers.

The fighting continued sporadically into May. While in the grip of one of his visions, Riel decided that the final battle was destined to be fought in Batoche, despite the risk to the families living there. Dumont protested, but once again gave in to his charismatic friend. The Métis prepared to meet the next attack in the town.

The assault came in two flanks, by river and by land. The odds were heavily in the Canadians' favour. But though the Canadians had the training, the cannons, and the machine guns, the Métis had Gabriel Dumont. He ordered his men to fight defensively; they dug trenches and set fires to confuse their enemy. His snipers kept their eyes peeled for the first glimpse of a red coat. Their tactics were successful at first, so there were relatively few Métis casualties. In the midst of battle, Riel walked around unarmed and unharmed, praying and brandishing a crucifix. "Oh, how hard it is to wage war!" he grieved.

But the battle soon became a siege. By May 12, the

Métis were running out of ammunition. Instead of shot, they crammed their hunting rifles with scrap metal and small stones. They melted down the lead from their tea chests to mould into bullets. Coffins were so scarce that the dead were sewn up in old blankets. The Métis soldiers were lucky if they had a few mouthfuls of food to keep them going. They lit their pipes at mealtimes, hoping the tobacco would stave off their hunger. The Canadians, meanwhile, had ample food and supplies. For the Métis, the situation was grim.

The Canadians continued to advance. Privately, Riel thought the town was lost. Though he was secretly contemplating surrender, he was still willing to bluff. In a letter to Middleton, he threatened, "If you massacre our families, we are going to massacre the Indian agent and other prisoners" who were being held at Batoche. Though Riel was worried about all the women and children in Batoche, he was particularly anxious about his own family. His wife, who had remained by his side, was pregnant with their third child.

White Flags at Batoche
It is estimated that Ottawa spent $5 million on the effort to quell this rebellion. Thousands of Canadian soldiers were dispatched by rail to the North-West Territories, to do battle with the poorly equipped Métis and Native

peoples. But the Métis had passion and desperation on their side. They were willing to give their all to the fight. The final battle, therefore, was also the most vicious. The newer soldiers, those patriotic Canadians volunteers, lost patience with their officers' cautious strategy. Defying Middleton's orders, they rushed towards the Métis, who scrambled out from their trenches to meet them. One after another, the Métis soldiers fell under Canadian gunfire. Métis casualties included a 93-year-old man. In a panic, one Métis turned to Riel and pleaded, "Work your miracle now. It's time." But Riel had no more miracles to work.

All was lost. White flags hung from every window in Batoche. But Riel and Dumont refused to surrender. After seeing his family to safety in a sympathizer's house, Riel ran to the nearby woods to meet Dumont. The two men knew it was useless to discuss strategy. "We are beaten," Riel panted. "We must die!" Dumont retorted. But the Métis resistance was broken. The last of the loyal Métis soldiers scattered into the trees as Canadian troops swarmed over Batoche.

The Canadian general sent word to Riel and Dumont that they would be offered protection if they, too, surrendered. "Go to the devil!" was Dumont's reply. "You tell Middleton that I am in the woods, and that I still have 90 cartridges to use on his men." He never used

Riel realizes his time is up and surrenders to a scout

those cartridges, and he was never captured. An old priest who knew Dumont well laughed at the idea of the soldiers ever finding him. "You are looking for Gabriel?" he asked. "You are wasting your time. There isn't a blade of grass in the whole prairie that he doesn't know."

Dumont left Batoche with nothing — and nothing to come back to. The Canadians had looted his house, then burned it to the ground. He didn't even have a jacket to keep himself warm. After Riel and Dumont had

The Incredible Adventures of Louis Riel

gone their separate ways, Dumont heard a rumour that his friend had surrendered. Disheartened, he fled across the U.S. border. He was never to see his "nephew" again. The rumour was true. After three days of dodging Canadian soldiers, Riel decided against trying to escape. He was almost 40, and no longer the young man who had eluded arrest and assassination at every turn a decade and a half earlier. "I will go to fulfill God's will," he said. On May 15, 1885, he approached a group of Canadian scouts and turned himself in.

Chapter 6:
The Trial of the Century

he rebellion had been crushed and the jails were full of defeated rebels. Big Bear and Poundmaker, leaders of the Native uprisings, had surrendered and were given speedy trials. They, and many of their men, were hanged without fanfare. Several key Métis soldiers were also awaiting their fate. Eventually, they were persuaded to plead guilty to their crimes, and were sentenced to varying prison terms. But the Mounties' biggest prize was still awaiting justice. Louis Riel was incarcerated in the North West Mounted Police barracks at Regina, Saskatchewan. They meant to deal harshly with this

"cur of a self-interested conspirator."

But Major-General Middleton, for one, was confused by their prisoner. Riel was hardly the firebrand he had been made out to be. Though prone to outbursts of religious mania, he was otherwise mild-mannered and would talk eloquently on many subjects. His appearance was also non-threatening. He no longer cut the bold, dashing figure he had as a young man. He was now hatless and sported a long, unruly beard. His clothes were dirty, and he wore an overcoat borrowed from Middleton. Only a pair of moccasins covered his feet. And a 20-pound weight fastened around his ankle prevented his escape.

The trial was scheduled to begin on July 20, 1885. Unlike the other rebels, Riel had no intention of pleading guilty. He was paranoid about being tried in English-dominated Saskatchewan and hoped instead that his case would be brought before the Supreme Court of Canada. It was true that the entire country was interested in his case. There was even a Riel Defence Committee in Quebec.

But Riel was not to get his national forum. He had committed his offences in the North-West Territories, and was to be tried in a Saskatchewan courthouse. Sympathetic French-Canadian supporters paid for his defence lawyers, who chose to defend him with the only viable defence. Despite Riel's protests, they planned to claim he was not guilty by reason of insanity.

They had a good case. His visions, prophecies, and erratic behaviour, as well as his incarceration in an asylum, all indicated long-term mental instability. Certainly, his current state of mind helped their claim. He vacillated between paranoia and confidence. At times, he seemed unaware of the gravity of his situation. He composed a letter to Prime Minister Macdonald, outlining his views of the future. He wished to take on a political role in Manitoba, he said, perhaps as a cabinet minister in some department. He seemed to have forgotten he might hang for his crimes.

Money, Power, and Blood

On the first day of the trial, the police were wary. They feared that the notorious rebel might escape. Though many of his co-conspirators in the rebellion had been arrested, several had gone into hiding. It was rumoured that Gabriel Dumont was plotting a daring daylight rescue of his much-revered leader. Three hundred mounted police were stationed in Regina. The air resounded with blasts from their bugles. A score of Mounties, clad in their distinctive scarlet uniforms, formed a tight ring around the courthouse. The small two-storey building could barely contain the crowd of people who wanted to watch the trial. Rich and poor alike had come to catch a glimpse of the "madman" who had defied a nation. They craned their necks to look at him as he stood in the prisoner's dock above them.

The Crown charged that "moved and seduced by the instigation of the devil" and "not having the fear of God in his heart," Louis Riel had committed treason against the Queen and the Dominion of Canada. Against the advice of his lawyers, Riel entered a plea of "not guilty." In his mind, he was innocent. Not once had he picked up a weapon, he reasoned. He wasn't even a Canadian citizen. How could he be guilty of treason? But he was not given the chance to defend his actions that day. To the disappointment of the crowd, the trial was adjourned for a week. The lawyers needed time to track down elusive witnesses, including psychiatrists who could to testify as to Riel's sanity, or lack thereof.

On July 28, 1885, the trial began in earnest. Judge Hugh Richardson presided. A jury of Riel's "peers" was selected. There was not a single Métis or a Francophone among them. While the Crown prosecutors explained that "money" "power" and "blood" drove him to commit his crimes, Riel remained calm and strangely confident. It was only when Charles Nolin appeared for the prosecution that he became agitated. His cousin's treachery still rankled. Riel seemed to fear a personal attack on his

Louis Riel (centre) addressing the jury during his
trial for treason in a Regina courthouse.

character. In defiance of court protocol, he jumped to
his feet and begged permission to speak. He exclaimed
that he had "200 questions" he wanted to ask, without
his lawyers' intervention.

Though the Crown was curiously willing to listen,
his defence team quickly moved to silence him. They
threatened to quit unless he behaved. "I cannot aban-
don my dignity," he said in protest, before lapsing into
silence. When the questioning proceeded, Riel's lawyers

were displeased by what they heard. Nolin revealed that he believed his cousin's messianic act was just that — an act. His testimony badly undermined the insanity defence.

Other witnesses, however, did not think Riel had been acting. Two of the priests Riel had clashed with flatly stated they thought he had taken leave of his wits. There was no other explanation for his outrageous behaviour, they stated. The more witnesses were called, the more confused the situation became. Some claimed he was deranged, others believed he was perfectly sane and knew exactly what he was doing when he defied the Canadian government. The psychiatrists were also divided in their opinions, despite the best efforts of the lawyers to pin them down. The bickering continued, back and forth. In summing up, Riel's defence offered a choice: Riel was either a "victim…of oppression or the victim of fanaticism." It was up to the jury to decide.

Finally, Riel was given the chance to address the court. It was the opportunity he had been waiting for. He had swayed hundreds of people with his passionate speeches in the past; surely he could do it again now. His life depended on it. Perhaps it was the suffocating heat, the strain of the drawn out proceedings, or his anxiety for his family, but he was not at his best. His speech did little to sway the jury. It was long, rambling, and peppered with religious references. The spectators, who had waited in so much anticipation, grew bored. His grandiloquent statements fell on unreceptive ears. "I know that through the grace of God I am the founder of Manitoba," he proclaimed. "I believe I am the prophet of the new world." It wasn't he who was insane, he charged, but the entire government of Canada. The jury then withdrew, to decide his fate.

While the jury was out, Riel knelt in the dock and began praying aloud. Some of the sensation seekers left. The case was not as exciting as they had hoped. There had been no dramatic testimony from surprise witnesses, no escape attempts, nothing but the dry legal wrangling of city lawyers. In seclusion, the jurors discussed the case. They were surprisingly sympathetic towards the Métis cause. But they did not believe the insanity defence. According to one of the jurors, Riel "seemed to us no more insane than any of the lawyers." They felt they had no choice. After only an hour, the jury filed back into the courtroom. With tears in his eyes, the jury foreman read the verdict aloud: guilty, with a recommendation of mercy. Riel stood, straight and silent for a moment, before bowing his head in defeat. In a case of treason such as this, a guilty verdict meant only one thing: Louis Riel would hang for his crimes.

Riel begged for the mercy of the court and

demanded another trial. "I have been hunted as an elk for fifteen years," he cried plaintively. Riel, and many others, suspected that the guilty verdict was retribution for the Thomas Scott incident. But the judge was adamant. "On the 18th of September next," he pronounced, "you will be taken to the place appointed for your execution, and there be hanged by the neck until you are dead, and may God have mercy on your soul."

Riel's lawyers, of course, quickly filed an appeal against the decision. During the ensuing legal wrangling, French and English Canadians continued to argue over Riel and his fate. Among the French, he was emerging as a kind of hero, an emblem of their struggle to maintain their identity. Among the English, however, anti-Riel sentiment was running high; the hangman had even offered his services for free. In Ottawa, Prime Minister Macdonald tried to placate both sides. "The conviction of Riel," he had initially declared, "is satisfactory." Riel's supporters in Quebec were furious. The wily politician then appeared to do an about-face and appointed a special commission to investigate his longtime enemy's alleged insanity. Three specialists were sent to examine him. Their findings were mixed; though finding him overly excitable on the subjects of religion and politics, he was lucid, even charming, in all other respects. It was enough for Macdonald. Riel was sane;

the verdict would stand. "He shall hang, though every dog in Quebec bark in his favour," he snapped. The date of the repeatedly postponed execution was now settled on. On November 16, 1885, Louis Riel would die.

In the time leading up to the execution, no less than five priests visited Riel. Under their guidance, he publicly renounced his heretical views. Privately, though, he continued to receive revelations and maintain that he was a prophet. He spent his days praying, fasting, and writing compulsively in his journal. He seemed resigned to his fate, but he was deeply concerned about the fate of his family.

When his mother, wife, and brother journeyed from Manitoba to say a final farewell, he broke down and wept. Who would take care of them after he was gone? He worried about the effect of his execution on his children and agonized over how they would handle the disgrace. He had other family concerns. Marguerite had given birth to their third child while he had been languishing in prison. The child was sickly and lived for only a few short hours. And his wife, who had never been robust, now had tuberculosis. Deeply troubled, he prayed: "Do not use the rope to draw me up to heaven." For the sake of his family, he was desperate to escape the noose.

Then, abruptly, Riel's worries vanished. "I am the

banner of the Lord," he wrote in triumph. "He bears me like a flag unfurled." He had had a glorious revelation. Christ would return in A.D. 4209, and he, Louis Riel, would be resurrected on the third day after his death. Death was no longer something to fear.

However, he was more circumspect in his final letter to his mother. "…the Lord is helping me to maintain a peaceful and calm spirit," he wrote. But it was difficult to maintain his composure with the hammering ringing in his ears. The gallows was being erected in an enclosure just outside his cell. He still felt he did not deserve such a fate. The only sin he had ever considered himself guilty of was gluttony. "A mouthful too much at our meals can only do us harm," he had lectured. All he requested for his last meal was three eggs.

On the morning of November16, Louis Riel was preparing to meet his God. He had spent all night in prayer; now he heard mass, gave his last confession, took communion, and received extreme unction, the last rite of a dying Catholic. "I die Catholic and in the only true faith" were the last words he wrote. At around 8 a.m., clutching a crucifix, and surrounded by priests intoning the "office of the dying," he walked calmly outside to the gallows. Even up to the last minute, the police expected a rescue attempt by Gabriel Dumont and Riel's other loyal followers. Fifty men surrounded the guardroom; another 40 waited by on horseback. But Dumont never came. Only a crowd of reporters and the curious came to watch the execution. Riel's hands were tied behind his back. "Courage, Father," were the last words he uttered to a weeping priest, before the noose was placed around his neck and the trap door released.

His corpse, in its wooden coffin, was returned to his mother. Hundreds of Métis filed through her house, paying their last respects to the man who, right or wrong, had furiously battled for their rights. Louis Riel was buried where he was born, on the shores of the Red River, in what had become the province of Manitoba, Canada.

Epilogue

Even after the execution, tragedy continued to strike the Riel family. Marguerite, Riel's wife, succumbed to tuberculosis within six months of his death. Angelique, their daughter, died of the same disease a few years later. Riel's long-suffering mother was left to bring up their remaining child, Jean. The boy did not inherit the rebellious spirit of his father and grandfather. He lived a blameless life under the pseudonym "Jean Monet."

Gabriel Dumont, Riel's loyal general, took a curious path. In the months after the rebellion, Dumont became a celebrity; he was even asked to join Buffalo Bill's infamous Wild West show. Surprisingly, he agreed. The Métis soldier posed for pictures, rode around in parades and showed off his sharp-shooting abilities in the ring. When his star began to fade, he was asked to leave. He eventually returned to Saskatchewan, where he died in obscurity in 1906, a year after the province entered Confederation.

Today, more than 100 years after his death, Louis Riel remains one of the most controversial figures in Canadian history. To some, he is a leader of almost saint-like proportions; to others, he is a madman and a

Epilogue

traitor to his country. Hero or villain, his deeds left an indelible mark on his country. He has been immortalized in songs and stories, poems and plays. Many still clamour for a pardon for this intense, enigmatic man known by so many names: the voice of a people, the prophet of a doomed cause, and, above all, the Father of Manitoba.

Bibliography

Bowsfield, Hartwell, ed. *Louis Riel: Rebel of the Western Frontier or Victim of Politics and Prejudice?* Toronto: Copp Clark Publishing, 1969.

Charlebois, Peter. *The Life of Louis Riel.*Toronto: NC Press, 1975.

Flanagan, Thomas. *Louis 'David' Riel.* Toronto: University of Toronto Press, 1996.

Flanagan, Thomas, ed. *The Diaries of Louis Riel.* Edmonton: Hurtig Publishers, 1976.

Riel, Louis. *Selected Poetry.* Toronto: Exile Editions, 2000.

Stanley, George F.G. *Louis Riel* Toronto: The Ryerson Press, 1963.

Woodcock, George.*Gabriel Dumont.* Edmonton: Hurtig Publishers, 1976.

Acknowledgments

The author acknowledges the following sources for the quotes contained in this book: *Louis Riel: Rebel of the Western Frontier or Victim of Politics and Prejudice?*; *The Life of Louis Riel*; *Louis 'David' Riel*; *The Diaries of Louis Riel*; *Selected Poetry of Louis Riel*; *Louis Riel*; *Gabriel Dumont*.

About the Author

Cat Klerks has a degree in English from McGill University and is the author of *Emily Carr: The Incredible Life and Adventures of a West Coast Artist*, also from Altitude Publishing. She lives and works in Banff, Alberta.

Photo Credits

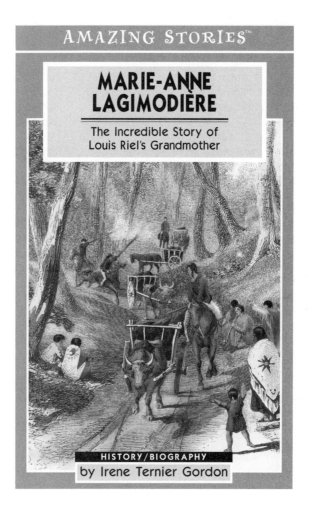

ISBN 1-55153-967-5

OTHER AMAZING STORIES

These titles are available wherever you buy books. If you have trouble finding the book you want, call the Altitude order desk at 1-800-957-6888, e-mail your request to: orderdesk@altitudepublishing.com or visit our Web site at www.amazingstories.ca

New AMAZING STORIES titles are published every month. If you would like more information, e-mail your name and mailing address to: amazingstories@altitudepublishing.com.